D0862055

BLOGGING ON INSTAGRAM

BLOGGING ON INSTAGRAM

Engagement Writing on One of the World's Best Social Media Platforms

Terri Nakamura

NEW DEGREE PRESS

BLOGGING ON INSTAGRAM

*Engagement Writing on One of the World's
Best Social Media Platforms*

ISBN

978-1-63730-447-1   *Paperback*

978-1-63730-551-5   *Kindle Ebook*

978-1-63730-552-2   *Digital Ebook*

This book is dedicated to my family and friends, my two cats, and my friends on Instagram.

Thank you for supporting me.

CONTENTS

INTRODUCTION 9

HOW TO USE THIS BOOK 15

CHAPTER 1 THE PATH TO BLOGGING 21

CHAPTER 2 ARE BLOGS STILL RELEVANT? 33

CHAPTER 3 WHAT IS ENGAGEMENT WRITING? 51

CHAPTER 4 REAL-LIFE ENGAGEMENT WRITING 67

CHAPTER 5 RULES OF ENGAGEMENT 85

CHAPTER 6 INSTAGRAM AS A DIGITAL DIARY 103

CHAPTER 7 WHY BLOG ON INSTAGRAM? 115

CHAPTER 8 CREATING YOUR PERSONAL BRAND 133

CHAPTER 9 IF YOU BUILD IT, THEY WILL COME 153

CHAPTER 10 LIGHTS, CAMERA, ACTION! 173

CHAPTER 11 FROM CAPTIONS TO CONTENT 191

CHAPTER 12 MAKE YOUR FEED AWESOME 205

CHAPTER 13 ARE YOU FEELING LUCKY? 225

CHAPTER 14 TIPS FOR BUILDING COMMUNITY 227

ACKNOWLEDGEMENTS 251

RESOURCES 257

GLOSSARY 269

APPENDIX 279

INTRODUCTION

You're under house arrest! That's how 2020 felt riding out a global pandemic. We were confined to our homes, cut off from our friends, and unable to communicate in real life with our colleagues. Video chatting helped reduce feelings of isolation and gave us ways to feel connected—like a "get out of jail free" card—but we needed more.

We had to search for silver linings. Some of us completed items on our "to-do" lists or tackled long-delayed home projects. We embraced online shopping and curbside grocery pick-up and figured out how to make the best of living without hairdressers. We even took up new hobbies, like baking bread or knitting, or we resurrected old ones like writing or taking photos.

The lockdown also presented an ideal opportunity to expand social circles in new ways, with channels we'd heard about but hadn't yet tried. We relied on these channels to keep up with friends, family members, and life in general. Social media made it possible to meet new friends in the US and worldwide and allowed us to safely "travel" without ever leaving our homes.

Social media also helped us conquer our feelings of isolation in 2020. One of the most rewarding and straightforward platforms is Instagram, a social media channel designed to share photos and captions. The "social" part of it is gratifying. Your community on Instagram can include a cousin in Topeka or a surfer in Sydney. It allows us to see the world through their eyes and learn about other countries and cultures.

Blogging on Instagram explores the intersection of social media and blogging, and by reading this book, you will find blogging on Instagram a positive—no, make that an "amazing"—experience. Blogging on Instagram is easy. Once you start, you'll find it's one of the best decisions you've ever made.

If you're someone who has been intimidated by the idea of launching a blog, this book is for you. It's for people who love to write and want to build an audience. It's for bloggers who are tired of writing blog posts that aren't found or read by others, or for those who want a place to share their words. Anyone can learn to use Instagram in this unintended way. This book will help "would-be" bloggers get their blogging feet wet and instill the confidence needed to one day launch a blog. Those who have no interest in starting a blog can choose to stay within the ease of Instagram as they pursue their writing journeys.

This book will help you with the process of creating effective blog posts and posting them on Instagram. It will help you master the learning curve to build and cultivate an audience for your writing. And, most importantly, you'll learn how to maintain the momentum and motivation to keep it all going.

Blogging on Instagram will help you in other ways as well. Suppose you like taking photos with your smartphone and haven't realized how to make your photos better. In this case, you will find advice about improving the quality of the pictures you shoot. Even if you're not a photographer, there are plenty of ways to express yourself visually on Instagram without a camera.

When I started using Instagram, I was new to shooting photos for myself. I'd had a long career as a graphic designer, working with dozens of professional photographers specializing in location, editorial, food, fashion, and product photography. I'd never fancied myself as a photographer, but when I opened my Instagram account and saw how good my photos looked using the built-in filters, I suddenly felt like a photographer with a personal online gallery. It was exciting to see my photos on display and even more fun when others liked them.

Blogging on Instagram is an entirely different experience. Compared with a traditional independent blog, there is very little to set up. It's available to use almost instantly, and there are no fees incurred.

Maybe you don't feel like you need a book to do this, but in learning to cook, I found it was easier to start with a recipe. Then, based on the outcome, I added some spices and left out ingredients to suit my tastes. So, in a way, you can think of this book as your Instagram blogging cookbook.

A change in my professional goals was the catalyst for me to use Instagram as a place to write. You don't know if anyone will read what you've written, but it feels therapeutic to share thoughts out into the void. I was rewarded for venturing into using the platform for writing. I didn't expect to receive so many significant and positive reactions, and at first thought it was random. But over time, I saw a correlation between longer posts and increased volumes of responses. As I continued to share blog-length posts, I experienced sustained growth and interest from my audience.

Research shows a growing trend in Instagram users posting longer narratives in captions. According to influencer marketing company Fohr, since 2016, the average length of a post has more than doubled to an average caption length of four hundred and five characters or about sixty-five to seventy words. Along with this growth has come increased engagement (Canning, 2020). Users have recognized that through the expression of thought, information, or instruction, they add value to their posts and receive more feedback from their audience. Besides straight-up photo sharing, there are various forms an Instagram post can take.

Instagram can be the place for your daily or weekly journal. For example:

- Foodies showcase places we can experience through their photos and descriptions.
- Others demonstrate cooking and baking how-tos and share recipes.
- Users broadcast information about issues affecting our world and attract like-minded readers.
- Creatives draw attention to their art, music, and crafts.
- Gardeners, animal lovers, and travelers share joy and wonder through updates to audiences near and far.

Content serves as a source of inspiration by providing images, videos, and stories that make us think and *feel*.

As I sat down to write this book, I wanted to understand more about this phenomenon. It was extraordinary because, as I started digging, I found evidence to support what I suspected: Posts with extended captions and longer narratives draw more substantial engagement, including a higher volume of quality interaction.

Why? Because followers read, relate, and when prompted, feel compelled to respond.

This book will show you how to use Instagram's pairing of visual and narrative content to start blogging. You'll learn how to use hashtags that will help people discover your content. Instagram offers an opportunity to have your words read by more people. You can use Instagram as a jumping-off point to encourage your audience to migrate to other properties, whether it be a blog, a brick-and-mortar store, or a business website.

I'm excited for you to try your hand at blogging on Instagram. Let's get started!

HOW TO USE THIS BOOK

———

The book focuses on Instagram, a platform that primarily exists to share visual content. The information reflects Instagram as of June 2021.

It's okay to skip around to find what looks interesting or valuable. As you flip through the pages, at the beginning of each chapter, you'll see key topics under the heading, "In this chapter."

The chapters start from an aerial view of content marketing, of which blogging has been a traditional tool, then they zero in on engagement writing. Social media channels such as Facebook, Twitter, and Instagram work similarly. Some conventions work across all of them, including some form of "liking" or saving a piece of content, commenting or engagement, and amplification through resharing a piece of content.

Other chapters focus on the mechanics and historical reasoning for considering social media channels as an outlet for your writing. For your convenience, there is a resource section and a glossary at the back of the book.

CHAPTER 1 –THE PATH TO BLOGGING

By learning how blogging fits into the marketing realm, you gain insight into the underlying benefit of blogging on Instagram. You have an opportunity to showcase your "value proposition," or promise, to your audience and deliver on their expectations through your writing. A brief history of marketing provides context about how blogging emerged as an outgrowth of the Internet. Marketing, blogging, and social media have paved the way for using Instagram as a blogging channel. Learn how writers share on the platform and its effectiveness as a blogging platform.

CHAPTER 2 – ARE BLOGS STILL RELEVANT?

This chapter provides an understanding of the origins of blogging. It discusses what it takes to set valuable goals. Learn about a blog's features and advantages and the financial and maintenance aspects of your investment. Consider when it makes sense to establish an independent blog versus a microblog, such as Instagram, and the differences between publishing on "owned space" versus "rented space."

CHAPTER 3 – WHAT IS ENGAGEMENT WRITING?

Engagement writing is the key to communicating and building a community on Instagram. By intentionally reaching out to your audience and asking them to share their experiences, thoughts, or opinions, you increase interaction. This framework can be applied in myriad ways when we communicate. We look at ways to cultivate engagement and examine how it differs from the interaction on a typical blog.

CHAPTER 4 — REAL-LIFE ENGAGEMENT WRITING

explains how the engagement in which we participate on Instagram can apply to other areas of our communications.

Engagement writing is essential on social media, but each day we encounter opportunities to communicate with people. Whether we're trying to schedule the plumber right away because we're having a gathering on Friday, or because we hope an Airbnb host can be flexible about pets, engagement writing can lead to satisfying outcomes. We learn how it's beneficial to extend it to all aspects of communicating.

CHAPTER 5 – RULES OF ENGAGEMENT

The reciprocal nature of social media is evident to many, but some of us need to learn about the expectations of giving and taking. Giving, in the form of feedback or acknowledgment, leads to making connections. You can take cues from the willingness of your audience to engage. You can figure out the kinds of stories you want to share and consider how to go about writing for interaction and building relationships. Whether you're interested in Instagram, Twitter, Facebook, or any other social media channel, the rules of engagement are similar. You'll learn how to enter these spaces and understand how to participate.

CHAPTER 6 - INSTAGRAM AS A DIGITAL DIARY

There are several ways to diarize on Instagram. This chapter explores how Instagram can work as a visual diary. Included are considerations for the type of content you might post, whether or not to make it public, the frequency of posting, and the types of imagery you might consider. Writing prompts offer ideas for your written content. If you're interested in taking your photos, there are suggestions about making them better.

CHAPTER 7 – WHY BLOG ON INSTAGRAM?

This chapter highlights some of our reasons to blog on Instagram and the benefits of doing so. You'll learn how limitations such as

SEO, search, backlinks, and data analytics work. If you experience limited post engagement on your blog, you'll learn how Instagram can reinforce your existing blog property. An ever present audience and instant, increased engagement are big reasons.

CHAPTER 8 – CREATING YOUR PERSONAL BRAND

First impressions matter. How do you want to be perceived? Transparency and trust are essential considerations when you create your presence on Instagram or any other social media. Begin with your username, avatar (profile photo), bio description, and information such as a contact email, website URL, or phone number. There are also ideas about themes and grids that can help you think about the look and feel of the content on your Instagram blog.

CHAPTER 9 – IF YOU BUILD IT, THEY WILL COME.

Instagram offers a two-pronged approach to getting attention. The first is the image, and the second is the caption or blog post. This chapter includes basics about image types, shooting, the apps you might consider using to enhance your photos, and options for sharing content. Learn why the first ninety characters of your post matter and ways to make your post readable and attractive. Find out what hashtags do and why they matter, and learn their benefits as well as how to tag your location or other users on Instagram. Understand how the algorithm works, and how interaction is "social proof" of an engaged audience.

CHAPTER 10 — LIGHTS, CAMERA, ACTION!

As if there isn't enough to think about, there's more! From its humble beginnings as a photo-sharing platform, Instagram has expanded its offerings both in image sharing and video. Those of you who are fans of Snapchat, TikTok, and livestreaming, have tools to express yourself directly within Instagram. This chapter includes information about Boomerang, Carousel, IGTV, Instagram Stories, Instagram Live and Reels. Your writing, image and sharing are first and foremost, but some of the newer content options could be useful in growing your audience.

CHAPTER 11 – FROM CAPTIONS TO CONTENT

This chapter explains how captions have taken center stage on Instagram. From 2016 until now, caption lengths have been growing and positively impacting engagement with readers and followers. In this chapter, you'll find information about the trends and metrics pointing to brands and key influencers that have recognized the value of microblogging and how you can use it to benefit your personal brand.

CHAPTER 12 – MAKE YOUR FEED AWESOME

Don't be intimidated if you aren't a visual communicator. Suppose you're new to blogging or want to get started on Instagram or other social media channels. In that case, a useful section of resources will make the most unartistic photographer feel that they can create a nice visual presence. There are many sources for visual imagery to support your writing, including stock photography, quotes, apps to help you convert a quotation into a graphic, as well as apps to help you make the most of your feed. This chapter has the potential to become a well-worn part of this book. There is space here to add your own resources as well.

CHAPTER 13 — ARE YOU FEELING LUCKY?

In the film, *Dirty Harry*, Detective Harry Callahan famously said, "You've got to ask yourself one question: 'Do I feel lucky?'"

CHAPTER 14 - TIPS FOR BUILDING COMMUNITY

There are a few simple things you can do to start your community on Instagram. Starting with your Facebook and personal contacts, you can begin by following people you already know. But how do you grow and sustain growth? Learn how engagement, hashtags, your posting schedule, and following specific types of people can make a difference as you build your community.

CHAPTER 1

THE PATH TO BLOGGING

IN THIS CHAPTER:

Content Marketing and Benefits of Blogging

It's Not Always About Search and SEO

Reaching Readers on a Personal Level

> *"Start telling the stories that only you can tell, because there'll always be better writers than you, and there'll always be smarter writers than you. There will always be people who are much better at doing this or doing that—but you are the only you."*

—NEIL GAIMAN, AUTHOR, AND PODCASTER

So how did we get here?

After World War II, mass media included print, radio, and TV. Together, these were used in advertising and marketing to push messages out to consumers. To ensure every consumer encountered a message, frequency (the repeated running of the same ads and commercials) amplified opportunities to ensure reach. Jingles and catchphrases helped drill a brand's message and product into a buyer's awareness. With the advent of the Internet, some businesses pivoted from broadcasting messages through a third party (such as an advertising agency) to directly publishing their content. Although the Internet allowed companies with small budgets to eschew the expenses of having an ad agency, talented people were needed to create the content, whether in-house or through outside professionals. Marketing on the Internet still focused on "push marketing," and the medium itself provided new ways to interrupt readers.

In *Wired,* Will Bedingfield says, "Before 1996, the web was a static, dull place. But the accidental creation of (Adobe) Flash turned it into a cacophony of noise, colour, and controversy, presaging the modern web." (Bedingfield, 2019)

Flash animations were persistent in demanding a website visitor's attention, and besides being annoying, Flash was known for exposing users to security vulnerabilities. Auto-playing videos and pop-up ads disrupted our online experiences. It was akin to how TV commercials interrupted our enjoyment of a television show. On the web, the solution was to use ad blockers to suppress unwanted messages. On televisions, DVRs made it possible to skip ads. But what if your content was not obnoxious or interruptive, and instead it created fans and followers?

CONTENT MARKETING AND BENEFITS OF BLOGGING

Seth Godin, a best-selling author and entrepreneur, is frequently quoted saying, "Content marketing is all the marketing that's left" (Pulizzi, 2008). He wasn't the first to think of this, but he highlighted a concept that began in 1895 with John Deere's *Furrow* magazine. *Furrow*, a journal for the American farmer, focused on the consumer with the intent to provide content that was wanted and needed. Farmers were among the first to benefit from content marketing, and today *Furrow* continues to offer readers information that informs, engages, entertains, and creates goodwill.

Content marketing is a strategic approach to the creation and distribution of relevant content. It is seen to be the most effective way to lead consumers to take a desired (and often profitable) action. With Instagram, the desired action is developing a following, and if you're blogging on Instagram, the initial goal is acquiring an audience for your words.

The content marketing approach naturally leads to relationships, and it has changed the way blogs are written and read.

Well-written content offers value. It shows how a customer's situation can be improved through a "widget," instead of extolling the virtues of the widget to sell more of them. By providing information of value, customer relationships and loyalty often follow.

> *"It isn't advertising. It isn't push marketing, in which messages are sprayed out at groups of consumers. Rather, it's a pull strategy. It's the marketing of attraction. It's being there when consumers need you and seek you out with relevant, educational, helpful, compelling, engaging, and sometimes entertaining information."*
>
> — REBECCA LIEB, CONTENT MARKETING ADVISOR

Through the use of content marketing, individuals and companies create opportunities to establish trust and authority and foster relationships through engagement with their audiences. Instagram provides a natural place to post content that has the potential to reach and gather brand loyalists.

Marketers view blogs as essential to improving visibility through search engine optimization (SEO). Fresh blog content increases the frequency of web indexing (where search engines "crawl" the web for keywords and metadata), because frequently updated content improves a web page's ranking and visibility. A typical blog post will contain 2–5 links (or more) to establish relationships with other websites, and the interconnectivity helps a website show up better in search engine results.

Blog posts are important parts of the purchasing funnel, where consumers can read, become aware, consider, evaluate, and eventually complete an action, such as a purchase or click. This is a "conversion." Instagram is in its own world, beyond the view of web crawlers. Instead of links, content is found through hashtags, so the path to conversion is different.

The differences between traditional digital advertising and marketing on Instagram contribute to a common discounting of Instagram (and other social channels) as blogging platforms.

I've been a blogger since 2005 and have enjoyed success on a personal level. My audience has been interested and engaged, and it has been an overall enjoyable experience. But being self-taught, I didn't understand "search engine optimization," keywords, links and "alt tags" (an invisible label to identify the contents of an image), or most of the plug-in features that can improve a blog's functionality and user experience. It wasn't until 2019, when I returned to college to study digital marketing, that I learned, among other things, how to build a WordPress site and became aware of how I could have implemented features that would make my blog(s) better and stronger.

For me, my limited visibility and success were gratifying even though they paled when compared to professional bloggers who blogged to earn a living. Generating an income from my blog wasn't my goal. I think a small percentage of people truly understand how to do this well, and a great many more, like me, start blogging without having a game plan and learn as we go. I wanted to have a place to write and to be read.

As we write to satisfy our reasons, we are marketing ourselves and our points of view, perhaps without even realizing it. We engage with those who visit our posts and hope they'll come back to read more.

I had an opportunity to interview Neal Schaffer, an authority on helping innovative businesses digitally transform their sales and marketing. While he agreed there might be people who use Instagram for blogging, and it may offer some functionality, it falls short. He said, "Short form media, such as Facebook or Instagram, have the ability to reinforce blogs because they remind people of your blog content. On Instagram, if people swipe up to your link, you can get them to visit your content. We're using social media to reinforce our blogs and perhaps it helps with brand awareness and helps us stay top of mind."

IT'S NOT ALWAYS ABOUT SEARCH AND SEO

According to writer Dave Schneider, a blog's essential goals are building traffic and building a mailing list (Schneider, 2021). It's possible to generate email sign-ups using Instagram, but it may be more beneficial to use your Instagram to direct traffic to your blog if you own a blog.

Instagram posts currently can't be found through search engines such as Google, Bing, or Firefox. However, within Instagram, small steps have introduced the search for keywords based on captions, content type, and location (where the content is shared). Search functionality will continue to improve and surface relevant content related to keywords that fall within the community guidelines on the platform.

Another perceived issue is the limitation of links on Instagram. A blog post will typically include up to five external links on a longer post (Bizzul, 2020). As of winter 2020/2021, there is still a limit of one link per post at the top of an Instagram account's home page in the bio section. From the standpoint of "backlinks," an SEO practice that helps with discoverability, the limitation of one link in the bio may seem restrictive. Still, given the quality of the traffic that results from that link to its destination, and the intentionality of the person clicking it, it achieves the goal of getting people to visit a website. Third-party services, such as Linktr.ee or Linkin.bio, enable a user to create a menu of relevant links, so it's possible to direct a reader to any that are listed.

Author and business consultant Ron Lichty shared great insight with me when he said, "All of us are marketing all the time. Some of us would do well to incorporate Instagram blogging into the marketing we do for products or services. Others of us are simply passionate about something. It's helpful to realize that when we write about our passion, sharing that passion is the equivalent of marketing."

Blog content can take many forms, and any content that allows you to engage with your audience can be a blog post. Social media, which includes microblogging on platforms such as Twitter and Instagram, has evolved from a fad to a fact of life. On the Internet today, it's estimated there are six hundred million blogs—an astonishing number! Tumblr alone accounts for 496.1 million blogs (Tankovska, 2020).

In 2021:

- Instagram reached 1.2 billion monthly active users.
- Facebook has 2.7 billion monthly active users.
- YouTube has 2.3 billion monthly active users.
- Twitter has a modest 353 million monthly active users (Kemp, 2021).

The reach of social media is ever-expanding and easily accessible, every moment of every hour of every day. Tapping into this "always present" audience is powerful.

To those who care about building or delivering to an audience, this kind of stuff is important. Research reveals a rich environment for entrepreneurs to connect with their niches and create a welcoming environment for writers who write for the sake of writing. While finding your voice and style of personal expression, you will discover the power and gratification in writing to an audience. Not only does this new kind of writing grow audiences, communities, and, most importantly, friendships, but it's also a great way to get real-time feedback on your thoughts. It's a handy way to crowdsource reactions to ideas quickly. It's hard to imagine any channel that does this better.

Recently, 1,865 people viewed an Instagram blog post I shared. Of the views, 294 people discovered my post via hashtags (the "#" symbols used to search for a topic or trending phrase). 212 people took an action on my post, including seventy-seven who clicked the link to a survey I wrote. I didn't initially set out to prove a point, I remembered one of the shortcomings of blogging on Instagram noted by several people I interviewed. Of the seventy-seven clicks, forty-eight people completed my nine-question survey, which represented a success rate of 62.2 percent. This level of follow-through, or conversion rate, was twenty times better than a typical "good" conversion metric of two-to-three percent (Kim, 2020).

Most people don't think of social media channels as blogging platforms because of how they have been used to share specific content categories. The perception is that the only blogs that are worthwhile are those we recognize as traditional independent blogs that offer SEO and related benefits.

Not all bloggers are in pursuit of conversions (the objective of getting readers to take the desired action). Author and B2B marketing strategist, Ardath Albee, says, "A conversation creates a more fluid experience for both parties based on increasing relevance with each exchange" (Albee, 2015). For some, the reward is the engagement and knowing an audience is reading and wants to participate.

REACHING READERS ON A PERSONAL LEVEL

I've seen a hunger for this type of writing. Instagram provides an environment where a user can establish a direct, and sometimes real-time, relationship with a writer. Through posts, comments, and conversations, intimacies often develop. This level of engagement is typically not found on a blog. There is a time lag between the time an article is posted on a blog and the moment a reader sees it. On Instagram, a post is seen instantly by *someone*. I've observed social media blogging to effectively direct followers to e-commerce websites and build lasting connections through shared content. I think most of us would agree it feels great to have a direct contact at a business. Channels such as Facebook and Twitter function as customer service access points. When posting a question or problem, businesses frequently respond immediately. Instagram makes it possible to achieve the same thing—providing audiences access to the person they want to communicate with—YOU.

As Instagram morphed from strictly a photo-sharing channel into a place where I could write and have my words read by more people than my blogs ever reached, it added value to the time, energy, and enjoyment on the platform. At first, I was surprised by the reactions. Unlike traditional blogging, social media channels, including Instagram, allow users to form genuine connections with people. They get to know you. They start to care about you. And if you're going through something and talk about it, they support you.

Thinking back to a time when I'd write a blog post, publish it, and sometimes wait hours or days to get a dozen comments, and comparing this to my blog posts on Instagram, where feedback is instantaneous, it's a no-brainer. Instagram is much more gratifying than any of my three blogs. The sensation of immediate engagement is worth sharing so others can experience the same kind of validation and support. Have you ever discovered something so cool you had to tell others about it? The response to blogs posted on Instagram made me feel a calling to write about it.

Whether you are new to blogging or social media or are an experienced writer or blogger, you'll be surprised at how easy it is to start blogging on Instagram and how much you enjoy it. You'll be blown away by the great people you meet and the things you see and read. You'll be able to establish personal connections with your audience and enjoy your interactions in ways that are rare on an independent blog.

By writing with openness, authenticity, and sincerity, I found the more I wrote, the more engagement I would receive. A blog post on Instagram doesn't need to be a certain length, but it needs to be long enough to get to your point. On my blog, if I received twenty comments, it was a runaway success. On Instagram, I started getting one hundred or even two hundred responses. Half of them were not substantive, but the ones that were began to add depth to my post, pushing whatever I wrote into a direction that gave me something back. Some of the comments were nearly as long as the post itself. I found these quite impressive.

I think this type of engagement writing is something a person can learn to do. I think people who start will naturally get better at it. In a short exchange with author and *New Yorker* columnist Louis Menand, he noted that when he first began contributing to *Slate*, an online versus traditional print medium, the editor, Michael Kinsley, said, "Write like you're writing an email." Instagram is a far cry from *Slate,* but by writing as if you're emailing a friend, you might just discover you've made one.

A key to succeeding on a digital channel is getting to know your community, expanding connections, and personalizing what would otherwise be impersonal mass communication. Through engagement writing, your original thoughts become more meaningful through contributions from others. You have an opportunity to interact with the audience you're writing to. It's a similar real-time interaction to the experience of receiving a "hello" back when we greet acquaintances on Twitter or Facebook.

If you are a writer, blogger, or social media marketer, you will find blogging on Instagram the most gratifying channel for expression and feedback. You'll see the difference between "rented media" (social media channels where the user doesn't completely control the channel) and owned media (such as a blog or website). Rented media isn't a deal-breaker because any audience built on Instagram has a better chance of migrating to other properties and channels. Metrics come along with this migration. Writing into a void is no fun, but writing to an audience that looks forward to your next post and is present when you publish it will reinforce the reasons you started writing in the first place—because you enjoy having people read your words.

CHAPTER 2

ARE BLOGS STILL RELEVANT?

—

IN THIS CHAPTER:

Blogging as a Communication Tool

Using Blogs to Monetize

The Blogosphere Grows and Plateaus

Blogging Hurdles

Owned Space versus Rented Space

When Does a Blog Make More Sense?

Why I Choose Instagram

BONUS: About Blogging on Instagram

"Blogs are an excellent way to understand the culture and direction of an organization."

TIM HUGHES AND MATT REYNOLDS, AUTHORS

When I started writing this book, I posed a question to Google: Is blogging still relevant in 2020? Interestingly, at the top of the search results, I found several posts that asked and answered the same question. Spoiler alert: They are.

Blogs, formerly known as "weblogs," have been around since the 1990s, and were found on sites like LiveJournal, where authors diarized their musings or published articles on topics of interest. Some blogs were based on a theme or content category and attracted readers who were searching the Internet for information on topics such as sports, politics, hobbies or reviews, advice (remember "Mommy blogs?") and more. In 2017, *The 1995 Blog* published a story about "15 of the most influential websites," and noted how "The Web … came to be recognized as a barrier-lowering, micro-targeting platform that could facilitate connections that otherwise would be difficult or impossible to achieve" (Campbell, 2017).

While many early blogs were based on personal opinion and thought, it wasn't long before businesses began to recognize the power of blogging as a way to grow their authority as well as increase sales. In *Epic Content Marketing*, Joe Pulizzi cites a famous example of successful content marketing. River Pools and Spas was a struggling company, selling a nonessential product, during the Great Recession.

In late 2009, the company began publishing blog posts focused on answering every conceivable question a consumer might have about fiberglass pools. It provided relevant and valuable information—the essence of content marketing. When a potential customer entered a related question into search, it invariably led to River Pools and Spas. Two years later the company sold more fiberglass pools than any other installer in the US, and its blog was attracting one hundred thousand unique monthly visitors (Pulizzi, 2014).

BLOGGING AS A COMMUNICATION TOOL

Blogging is an essential tool in content marketing. I'm not a marketing writer, so I'm coming at you with a different spin than experts in the social media marketing realm.

Still, I acknowledge how content marketing offers something of value to a reader and understand how it gets people to read and connect with a brand, all the while laying the groundwork for making a sale or getting readers to take a desired action.

A completed action is known in marketing parlance as a "conversion," and can take many forms—from requesting a download, signing up for a newsletter, asking for more information, or making a purchase, among other actions. I can't tell you how many times I've freely given my email address in exchange for a white paper, report, or other tangible item. Content marketing is an important way for businesses to reach potential customers and is frequently delivered to consumers in the form of a blog post. But conversion is also possible on Instagram. And because of the instantaneous interaction that takes place there, it's a more powerful platform for engagement.

USING BLOGS TO MONETIZE

In the 1990s, it wasn't unusual to see sponsored content that appeared in the guise of impartial recommendations. As social media took center stage, it was important to protect consumers from accepting what they perceived as unbiased information that was specifically created to influence purchasing decisions.

To clarify guidelines for transparency, the FTC released endorsement, testimonial and sponsored content guidelines advising disclosures in advertising. Whenever I saw links in the body of a blog post, it always gave me the impression that the blogger was making it easy for me to find a product or service. I didn't realize clicking on a link was a way for the blogger to earn commissions on sales of the products or services they promoted. The FTC, to help protect consumers and ensure fair business practices, mandated affiliate link disclosures. You have probably noticed statements such as, "If you buy a product through our posts, we may be paid a small portion of the sale."

Affiliate marketing is the selling of goods and services through links placed in blog posts and on websites and was patented in 1989 by William J. Tobin. Affiliate networks such as ClickBank and Commission Junction have been kicking around since the late 1990s. In 1996, Amazon launched its Associates Program which allowed bloggers to earn commissions through the placement of affiliate links on their blogs and websites.

Google launched AdSense in 2003. This program places ads on sites that target certain audiences and gives bloggers a chance to make money whenever a visitor clicks or views an ad. In 2011, a blogger and SEO expert told me how he would write posts in response to search queries and get enough clicks on ads to make tens of thousands of dollars each year! Suddenly a blog wasn't an indulgence or hobby—it became a source of income! By 2020, affiliate network marketing grew to be a $12 billion global industry (Rastas, 2021).

Blogs became channels to reach niche audiences. Bloggers were enlisted to amplify information about a product or service and readers would trust the source because it was content, not an advertisement. Think about Amazon reviews and how you're influenced to buy a product based on the ratings and reviews. I used to feel it was my duty to review purchases to let others know if a product was good or not. Blog recommendations carried weight in the same way, while the affiliate links in them helped bloggers make money.

According to Hubspot, around 2010, eleven percent of bloggers made their primary sources of income from their blogs.

In 2017, the FTC updated its page to show influencers how to comply with the requirement to identify paid or sponsored content. The simplest way was to append "#Ad" to a post. There will be times on Instagram where you'll see the "#Ad" hashtag, but to increase transparency even more, Instagram encourages the acknowledgement of partnerships through the designation of sponsored content (Brownstein Hyatt Farber Schreck, 2020).

I wrote blog posts focused on Verizon Wireless and various technology products or services and disclosed sponsored partnerships through OM Media Group, an influencer marketing agency with access to more than five thousand active US content creators, influencers, streamers, gamers, bloggers, and storytellers from all walks of life. Very early on, OM Media demonstrated leadership in best practices regarding transparency, to the point of allowing bloggers to share their views, even if they were critical.

THE BLOGOSPHERE GROWS AND PLATEAUS

Blogging platforms like Blogger (founded in 1999, and now owned by Google); WordPress (founded in 2003, now owned by Automattic); and Tumblr (founded in 2007, and now owned by Verizon Media) are still viable. I still have blogs on all three of the platforms! But many platforms have gone by the wayside. Some of you might remember your favorites, such as Myspace, which has become irrelevant, or Posterous and Geocities, which have vanished forever.

As some platforms disappeared, others came to the forefront and in 2004, Pew Research reported six million Americans were getting their news and information from blogs (Rainie, 2005). According to former blog authority Technorati, there were fifty million blogs by July 2006 (Chapman, 2011). That meant the blogosphere had doubled in size about every six months and was one hundred times larger than it was in 2003 (Sifry, 2006).

Since that time, the options to publish have multiplied to include microblogging on social media sites including Twitter,

Facebook, Pinterest, Instagram, and others. As blogging options have proliferated, there are many more options for creating and discovering content.

Blogging will remain an important component of marketing, but in recent years it has receded as a hot topic. Until I began writing this book, I didn't realize that there is a lingering concern about the demise of blogging. A 2015 post by Blog Tyrant is called, "Is Blogging Finally Dead?" Apparently, I'm not the only person who wondered. A recent update by Konrad Sanders posed the question: Are Blogs Still Relevant in 2020? He acknowledged it's a time-consuming effort to do it well. He goes on to describe all the reasons why yes, blogs are still relevant.

BLOGGING HURDLES

There are several hurdles to jump when starting a blog, starting with the platform. Some you've maybe heard of: Medium, WordPress, Blogger, Typepad and others. Some are rented space, but others offer the ability to host your website or options to access more features.

When starting an independent blog, one needs to decide on a domain name and secure a host, which together form the information that will lead people to the Uniform Resource Locator, or URL, that most people recognize as a web address. That's the beginning.

Choosing a suitable domain name takes time and thought. Many of the names you can think of have already been taken. I can remember searching and feeling frustrated that I couldn't find what I wanted, only to have the hosting company make awful suggestions by adding "The," some other prefix or suffix, or "extension."

Top-level domains such as "dot.com," "dot.net," or "dot.org," are the most respectable, but "dot.com" is always going to be the winner. You can opt for a "non-dot.com" domain but it's best to avoid extensions associated with spam. A few of the worst domains include "dot.surf," "dot.date," and "dot.cam," but myriad others sound … iffy. You can check Spamhaus. org, which fights spam on the internet, and offers a list of the worst domains based on which ones send out the most spam emails (Spamhaus, 2021).

Domains can be inexpensive and are available through tons of domain name registrars. Some well-known registrars are GoDaddy, BlueHost, HostGator, and WP Engine, but there are others that are unfamiliar and less costly.

You'll need to find a web host. What does a host do? It provides servers that power and store your website. Some offer packages that include website builders and "dashboards" that provide tools you need for building a site, posting content, and optimizing it for search, among many other functions. The process is a lot easier now than it used to be. It's possible to choose from website starter templates and quickly and inexpensively cobble together a site, although to someone who is unfamiliar with the terminology or even understanding the point of WHY anyone would want to do this, it could be daunting.

If you hire a web developer and designer, they will be able to help you. But why would anyone who is just dabbling in the realm of blogging undertake the time and expense of hiring a designer or a developer?

If your goals include e-commerce or a business website, or you want to create a blog for affiliate marketing purposes, a developer and designer will be able to create a professional brand presence.

Because time and money are needed to create and sustain a blog, a number of questions surface. Both an independent blog and a company blog need someone to write the content and post it, as well as monitor and respond to interactions. Who will be responsible for the site maintenance and troubleshoot when something breaks? Another piece—who will actively publicize it through social media and mailing lists? Who will chase the audience?

As the owner of three independent blogs, I can attest to the time it takes to keep them running smoothly. I love technology, but I've never loved troubleshooting problems on my blogs.

At this point, if you are still thinking about creating a full-featured, independent blog, you'll most likely still want to have an Instagram account. If you're putting any kind of effort into your Instagram posts, there is always an opportunity to cross-post teasers from Instagram to your blogging property. Any visitor who migrates from your Instagram post to your actual blog adds value to the post you've already worked hard to craft.

Marketers and bloggers are committed to the value of a blog, but I've seen Instagram users break the script and fashion their Instagram feeds into successful blogs in their own right.

A blog is an important component of any website because it increases the chances of having the website turn up in search results. Blog posts require time and energy, so modifying your post to share on Instagram could take advantage of the work you've already done. As of June 2021, your Instagram profiles are indexed by search engines such as Google, Bing, and Yahoo, and will turn up when searched, but Instagram posts and images won't be found (Facebook, 2021).

When a person enters a search query, they want useful and fast results, so relevant content is important. Frequently updated pages that are relevant and incorporate criteria such as keywords, alt tags, readability (subheads, limited paragraph lengths, active nouns and more) help ensure a blog post will be crawled and delivered as a search result. A blogger's goal is to show up on the first page of organic search results, because they're the most often clicked.

In the Blog Tyrant post, Google Trends revealed a decline in search interest for "blogging" over the course of roughly fifteen years. It seemed to peak sometime around 2006–2008. I found this curious and decided to conduct a Google Trends search for "blogging" (April 22, 2020) and found a downward trajectory between 2004 and 2018. And over the past few years, it has been in a holding pattern as it continues a gentle decline.

I wondered what would happen if I did a head-to-head comparison of "blogging" and "Instagram," and I found anywhere from 70 to 100 percent growth of Instagram over blogging during that time frame. While the term "blogs" has flattened, "Instagram" has enjoyed rising interest. We've learned blogs are still relevant, but they appear to be losing steam. Are some bloggers starting to realize the juice isn't worth the squeeze?

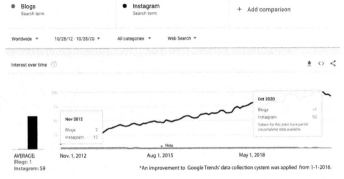

Google Trends comparison shows the volume of searches for "Blogs" versus "Instagram" over 8 years. Chart by Terri Nakamura | Data source: Google Trends (https://www.google.com/trends)

OWNED SPACE VERSUS RENTED SPACE

Owning an independent blog allows creators to control the fate of their content.

Blogging on free platforms such as Blogger and Tumblr or microblogging on Twitter and other social media channels are, in the words of Neal Schaffer, "rented space." In other words, the content posted on them is yours, but it lives there at the will of the site. Users of the platform Posterous (2008-2013) might recall how the trendy and beautifully designed blogging platform offered ease of use, analytics, and integration with other sites, but when it died, the content there died with it. I felt the pain because I had a Posterous blog and when it shut down. I didn't realize my posts would be lost forever.

WHEN DOES A BLOG MAKE MORE SENSE?

Rented space on social media has two immediate advantages: It's easy to use, and it's free. From multinational companies to the hobbyist, all will agree rented space isn't necessarily a drawback. Consider YouTube: Each minute, four hundred hours of content is uploaded to YouTube. Its search engine is second only to Google's, and 62 percent of businesses maintain a presence there (Mohsin, 2021). It doesn't appear anyone is worried because they don't own the space.

There are reasons a blog makes more sense. For businesses, a blog is an essential part of a company website to increase the chances of being discovered in search. Blogs are effective channels for providing value to their readers and for creating opportunities to engage audiences and convert visitors to customers. In terms of marketing, a blog is often considered an essential tool in the marketing toolbox.

If writing and branding yourself or your services is your goal, a blog may be what you need. A few reasons you might consider creating an independent blog include:

- You have a purpose for your writing, such as posting articles that establish you as a thought leader in a particular niche;
- You may be writing to generate an income through links; or
- You want to support your business by enhancing its visibility through search.

If you are interested in blogging, ask yourself what your motivation is and how committed you are to making it succeed. And consider whether you have the time or financial resources to invest in creating and maintaining it.

On a blog, maintenance issues can be vexing. By comparison, maintenance of a social media channel is not your problem. Blogs require effort to draw eyeballs, while social media audiences are constantly tuned in.

WHY I CHOOSE INSTAGRAM

For me, blogging was an outgrowth of my interest in social media. In the early 2000s, everyone was doing it. I've personally started three blogs since 2005. None were high profile, but the one I invested the most time in has had a half-million cumulative views. I was proud of the views, but none were in the realm of a serious blog. I didn't have a clear purpose with any of them. Why did I start a blog? Because I wanted to have a place to post my writing.

Since my goal was simply to write, making money wasn't a motivator for me. I earned a good living from my graphic design business, so I think it would be accurate to say that as a blogger, I was a dilettante.

My first blog, *Confessions of a Graphic Designer*, had a small and loyal following of active readers, and thrived as long as I continued my commitment to generate new posts. With each new update, I'd share the link with family, friends, as well as Twitter and Facebook where my largest audiences lived. The posts would receive a good number of comments, and even back then, I would respond to each one. Around 2013, OM Media was looking for social media denizens with good followings who actively engaged with their audiences. They invited me to join a group of social media influencers, many of whom were at the forefront of social media in its nascency.

Instagram posts have fewer "moving parts." Over the years, for me, blogging began to feel like a chore. It took a lot of time for me to write a blog post. The writing itself was one thing, but there were also "un-fun" parts like adding links, finding, buying, or creating images, and checking over and over for mistakes to make sure all the pieces were there and working correctly. Even when I thought it was a simple post, I'd find myself revising it ten times. Hitting the "publish button" was anticlimactic. I could wait hours or days for someone to view, like, or comment.

On both blogs and Instagram posts, it's possible to fix a typo or make a correction in the blink of an eye. On an independent blog, its subscribers receive the blog post via email in the originally published state, so if you've made an error, it lives on in the email. I sometimes correct an Instagram post within moments after I've published it because I'll notice a mistake. Once it's corrected, there's no evidence it ever happened.

Throughout history, writers have written, not necessarily because of the lure of making money, but because it fed the soul. It offered an opportunity to express thoughts and ideas, entertain, make people think, and earn praise. I believe personal reasons are often the most motivating, and sometimes, "if you write it, they will come." You'll learn how it happened for one Instagram blogger in the following bonus content.

BONUS: ABOUT BLOGGING ON INSTAGRAM

Jonathan Buyno (@jonathanbuyno) is an Instagram blogger with 17K followers. His first post on Instagram coincided with starting photography—October 23, 2019. Within two months of opening his account, he began sharing long-narrative blog posts, and when he did, his engagement increased to hundreds of comments and thousands of likes. He is a self-taught photographer and takes beautiful photos as he lives and travels in his jeep. His posts are personal, reflective, and draw meaningful responses from his audience. As of mid-2021, he engages sincerely with all comments.

Has blogging on Instagram helped you personally? When I first left on my travels, I didn't have a clearly defined path. I was trying to reconnect with myself after the Marine Corps and wanted that sense of freedom to go out and do something on my own. When I started photography, I was good at it, and I was getting all this praise. I was doing something that I loved, and that's when I packed up my house and left. At first,

I didn't write too much, but then one day I started feeling more secure about sharing whatever was on my mind. I felt Instagram was like my journal. I like that I can go back and look at a photo and it brings back a lot of memories.

Did you consciously realize that Instagram could be a business platform for you? I've had people email me about partnerships, but I haven't done one because I don't want to change the message I'm sharing. I'm not trying to sell anything to anybody.

What has been the biggest benefit to you since you started on Instagram? The biggest benefit is the sense of calmness I feel. As time went on, I found a beauty within me where I realized once you remove the layers in your life, there's peace. I follow my intuition in my photos and few of them are planned. Some are taken on the side of the road or on top of my jeep. I try to go with the flow a lot more now, so that's a big change with me. I'm more connected with myself.

What would your advice be to someone who is interested in using Instagram for blogging? I would say that they should. What works for me is to be one hundred percent yourself, and don't try to win people over. Be yourself because you're going to attract people who vibe with you. The problem is when you're trying to fit in. I'm not saying push boundaries, but when you're doing something and it's yours, sometimes you might feel uncomfortable with writing about it, but for me, that works. Build your audience, and just know that not everyone is going to be a fan, and that's okay. What you're trying to do is reach the people who align with whatever you're trying to do, whether that's selling, blogging, or offering advice. You know you're searching for those people, so I just think about being authentic—being real. Being yourself and doing it for yourself.

Monetizing can affect how people feel about you. Do you see power as something you would have to use carefully? I feel like you give a little bit up, and you would want to make sure that it's the right decision. If down the road I was able to partner with a reputable company, and if we could do something good with that money, that would be good. I grew up very poor. There was one person who brought Christmas presents to all six of us kids. Last December I helped someone out like that. I like to give back because one little thing that you do—you don't know how it's going to affect somebody else. It's true.

CHAPTER 3

WHAT IS ENGAGEMENT WRITING?

———

IN THIS CHAPTER:

What is Engagement Writing?

Comments Are the New Eye Candy

Instagram versus Blog Engagement

How is a Post Found?

Visibility Leads to Greater Engagement

Sharing to Other Channels

Benefits of Engagement Writing

Bonus: Example of Engagement Writing

"Communication is a skill that you can learn. It's like riding a bicycle or typing. If you're willing to work at it, you can rapidly improve the quality of every part of your life."

—BRIAN TRACY

L et's say Oprah calls and wants to interview you. You're excited because it's *Oprah*, and even though you don't know what she'll ask, the promise of an interesting conversation is anticipated. You look forward to answering her questions and sharing your thoughts. The same appeal is at the heart of engagement writing.

WHAT IS ENGAGEMENT WRITING?

Engagement writing inspires interaction with your reader and cultivates connections through communication. In the best case, it can lead to an exchange of comments and replies, giving your readers a chance to get to know you and for you to get to know them. The trust that develops from these conversations can lead to achieving goals, whether they include the reader clicking a link, becoming a subscriber, or lengthening the time they spend on your website. Using engagement writing in blogging and social media increases your chance to earn a comment, like, share, or conversion.

Engagement writing occurs naturally when your audience is interested in you or your content. For example, your post can explain how to do something, describe a recent experience, or share a funny story. Whatever the subject matter, you can do two things when writing your posts:

- Meet your writing objective to describe, inform, or entertain.

- Invite your reader to participate in your story.

Interactions with your readers lead to establishing relationships in social media, with coworkers, or with people in your orbit, and they allow for the development of more touchpoints to reinforce those connections.

On Instagram, you're not writing to an individual—you're writing to an audience. Through relatable content, you make them feel like you are writing to each of them. If you invite opinions or reactions, your readers understand and willingly respond.

COMMENTS ARE THE NEW EYE CANDY

More people are interested in authentic conversations with real people in real time. According to a story about Instagram that appeared in a recent issue of *The Atlantic:*

> *"In a world where everyone's photos look the same, comments are what keep posts interesting [...] and recently, Instagram comment sections have begun to eclipse the photos they sit below."*
>
> — *TAYLOR LORENZ*

Engagement is an essential part of audience building. Just as it's true on a blog, the comments we receive on Instagram posts are the lifeblood of any story that is shared. Comments are the new eye candy on Instagram. In a sea of flowers, animal photos, and landscapes, comments oftentimes deliver additional value to our readers.

But how can you write a post that inspires viewers to comment? And how do you keep the conversation going? We discuss ways to do this in Chapter 5, "Rules of Engagement."

INSTAGRAM VERSUS BLOG ENGAGEMENT

In print media, writers hope their words affect their readers, but there are limited ways to gauge how deeply their words resonate. By posting on a blog, it's possible to see how many times a post is visited and for how long, and the number of comments that are left.

On a blog, comments are the result of several factors including the length and structure of a post, the size of the audience (subscribers and sharing to social channels), and a "call to action" (also called a CTA).

On Instagram, users can instantly view the engagement they receive on their posts through the number of likes and comments, and Instagram business accounts can drill down further to find metrics about their audience.

VISIBILITY LEADS TO GREATER ENGAGEMENT

The ease of quickly creating a community is a significant reason that blogging on Instagram is such a game-changer.

Assuming you've begun following people, following back, and actively engaging with the content you see, your blog posts on Instagram will be seen immediately and receive feedback. It offers instant gratification—something that isn't typical on a blog.

Being visible to others is a huge part of creating opportunities for engagement. Although it takes time on a blog, building a community on Instagram can take place relatively quickly. One way to kick-start your community when you create your account is by adding your Facebook contacts. (More info on growing your community in Chapter 14.) Once you've acquired some followers, there are two key visibility metrics:

- **Impressions** are the number of times your content (posts or stories) is presented to users.

- **Reach** reflects the unique number of users that viewed your post or story on a given day.

Your engagement activity on Instagram affects how many people can view your post. To calculate your engagement rate, divide the number of likes by the number of followers, then multiply by one hundred.

> **Engagement rate example:** An account with ten thousand followers has five hundred likes, so the engagement rate is calculated by dividing five hundred by ten thousand. The engagement rate, in this case, is 5 percent.

Instagram is inclined to show your content to more people if the algorithm identifies it as something viewers would like to see. So the higher the ratio, the more your content will be visible. If the algorithm determines the content is not going to interest viewers, it's shown to fewer people.

When you're a little-known blogger, acquiring subscribers is a slow process. When you write a new post and send out notifications, you cross your fingers and hope someone will read it, like it, or leave a comment. The process doesn't consistently deliver results.

Most blogs have a subscription feature to help build an audience. A visitor subscribes to a blog and receives a notification when there is a new post. Subscriptions work well when the content is meaningful, timely, and changes frequently. I like news aggregators like *TechCrunch* or art blogs like *Colossal*. The downside is, when I'm busy, subscription notifications can end up in the trash, or on rare occasions, I mark subscriptions as spam or block them to get them out of my inbox.

Subscribers are essential assets and needed to increase the flow of traffic to a blog. The more you have, the greater the chance of someone reading your post. It's possible to build a list relatively quickly by deploying pop-ups, offering incentives such as access to a download, and simply buying traffic.

But on Instagram, it's a much simpler process. And when we use Instagram, our audience *chooses* to be there.

HOW IS A POST FOUND?

On a blog, before someone can read or react to your post, they must be able to find it. Practices used in writing blog posts make them more likely to be found through search engine optimization (SEO). There is more about SEO in Chapter 7.

I've often opened a link to a blog post that has been carefully written, researched, and optimized, but has few or no comments. As a blogger, I know how much effort is required, so when a post gets zero or very little feedback, it can feel disheartening.

Instagram creates opportunities to find readers because the nature of the platform is the discovery of content. Users search for topics of interest using Instagram's internal search. Are you looking for inspiration, beauty tips, or marketing help? Do you like cars, goats, or gardening? You can find almost every type of content on Instagram.

The bigger the audience, the greater the chances to be seen and engage. Unlike blogs, that rely on subscribers to get views, on Instagram, your post goes live the moment you publish it, and you don't sit on pins and needles waiting for reactions because your audience is already there, waiting for it.

When a post is shared over other social media, sharing increases the odds of being discovered, depending on the channel and the number of followers one has. On Instagram, users have the option to instantly share their posts over to Twitter, Facebook, and Tumblr (another blogging platform). Followers on those channels can be exposed to your post.

Sharing to Other Channels

- The half-life of an Instagram post is nineteen hours, but it often gathers engagement for several days (Epipheo, 2020).

- According to Sprout Social, a piece of content shared on Twitter has a lifespan of fifteen to twenty minutes (West, 2020).

- Post Planner says a Facebook post reaches its peak exposure in fewer than three hours (Ayres, 2016).

- Tumblr's life span is not available. However, it has a unique ability to "reblog" which acts as a signal boost so your post can continue receiving exposure. (As of June 2021, Instagram continues to allow auto sharing an Instagram post to Tumblr.)

BENEFITS OF ENGAGEMENT WRITING

On Instagram, engagement writing helps you create a personal connection with your followers, so even unattractive posts can receive likes and comments simply because *you* are posting them. When people see their friends, they're inclined to be supportive and will like and comment on ordinary, extraordinary, and even unattractive content the moment a post is published.

Those who enjoy writing have a chance to build a community of fans and friends using Instagram. When we connect directly with our audiences, we receive feedback right away.

The immediacy is satisfying—especially if you're used to blogging and the usual delay from the time you post to the time you receive responses. You'll receive comments that don't add value, but those who have opinions or reactions and share them with you validate the reasons for sharing in the first place.

By inviting your audience to weigh in, you can crowdsource opinions, conduct informal research, and gain insights into your communities. If asked, audiences are ready to offer you feedback.

Using Instagram as a blogging platform is a safe way to put yourself out there, learn what works, and improve your processes, all while building a following and experiencing what it's like to be a part of a global community.

Now that we understand engagement writing, the next chapter tells us how to do it!

BONUS: THE BITCOIN POST—
AN EXAMPLE OF ENGAGEMENT WRITING

My images don't always illustrate my blog post because I'm aware there are two layers of attention on Instagram.

- **The first layer is based on the merits of the image**—whether it's interesting, unique, or visually appealing. (Note: sometimes images are NONE of these things but will be liked and receive comments because the person posting it has a community of supportive fans who will like anything that is shared regardless of merit.)

- **The second layer of attention is the "teaser"**—created within approximately the first ninety characters of your caption (including the number of characters in your username). When I designed magazines, I often placed teasers on the cover to get readers interested in the stories inside. The first few words of your Instagram blog post function that way. It's a chance to draw your audience into your blog post. (You'll learn more about this in Chapter 5.)

The sample post below received 1,324 "likes" and 415 comments. It is the weirdest post I've ever shared on Instagram, and the comments were more than average. Note: I posed a question in the first line and wrote about a topic that concerns many of us.

Have you ever received a ransom email? It happened to me 3x this week. An old LinkedIn password was in the subject line. It was scary!

The email threatened to publicly release private videos of me if I didn't pay $2K in Bitcoin!

No such videos exist, but it still shook me up. I also thought: "Bitcoin? How does it work?"

IMAGINARY CONVERSATION:

ME: Hello, CREEP. I read your email with great interest. In the video of me—am I doing something REALLY naughty? I can't wait to see what you found! Are you sure it's ME? I know you're just trying to make a dishonest living here, but there's a problem: I don't know how to use Bitcoin. Can you help?

CREEP: Are you living in a cave? Everyone knows how to use it!

ME: Um, sorry, no. No idea.

CREEP: Unbelievable. OK, I'll make a YouTube tutorial for you & mark it "private," then send a link.

Later—

ME: Thanks for the link. The tutorial was great! I think I get it! BTW, I liked it & subscribed to your channel & left a comment. Also, I added it to my "Favorites" & "Watch later" lists! Bitcoin seems risky, though. Can't I just use PayPal? It'd be way easier. Also, you found me on LinkedIn & I guess for obvious reasons you didn't send me a connection request.

CREEP: I can't believe this. Y'know what? Just forget it. And I'm taking down the video.

ME: No! Please don't! It was REALLY well done. You should make it public! It'll get lots of views, likes & comments AND you might inadvertently receive thousands in Bitcoin from unsuspecting idiots! Just make sure to add tags to it!

CREEP: I'm blocking your email address. Don't contact me again.

ME: You didn't say "please."

NOTE: #StaySafe. This is written in jest, but #Ransom emails are on the rise. TIP: Use email preview, then block the senders & mark as #Spam. #Scammers want to make $ during #Lockdown

EXAMPLES OF ENGAGEMENT ON THE "BITCOIN RANSOM" POST

Often a follower will see a post and leave a comment, and the comment will receive no response. Responding to a comment with more than an emoji leads to more interesting interactions. When give and take happens periodically, we get to know people in our audience, and start to form friendships. A thoughtful response shows our appreciation for their time and engagement.

@queenhorsfall Omg my friend got a similar email yesterday, but they asked for $500 in bitcoin. She does have bitcoin plus email was written like a translation from English into Russian. I get a lot of spam to my Hotmail email, but not google.

> **My reply:** The first one was freaky, Diana. On the other two I found myself wanting to correct their grammar and spelling. Clearly, they were having a bit of fun with it as well!

@lady_ofshalott_ Such a funny story, Teri. I received a ransom mail two weeks ago with about the same content and had to change my password everywhere. It took ages.

My reply: …I thought maybe it was mostly happening in the US, but it sounds like it has happened in other countries. I've been changing passwords, too, which was probably necessary based on this episode!

@fragrant_soil Wow! Scary! What the hell is happening all over? Glad you negotiated that minefield!

My reply: …Jas, I think there must be some kind of an underground exchange where information is traded and used by people. The opportunists figure the more often they try the better their chances that one person will respond?…

@hadels.maayeh Yes, I got a lot of bribes…of videos and so-called porn….LOL! There are more thieves trying to scare you and for you to pay in bitcoin. I report and block them. Just keep doing that and ignore the emails.

My reply: …I guess some people report the spammers but honestly they're probably using fake email addresses so I can't see how it would be very useful. Blocking and trashing is good!

@photogrrl67 Have to tell you I've been getting those emails too! But couldn't figure out where they got the password but your reference to LinkedIn made me go "AHHA!" I laughed at it when I got it (have gotten a few times) and had the same fantasy thought of egging them on. Thanks for the laugh. Blocking and deleting here, too.

> **My reply**: …something I noticed about the email was that. It look[ed] like the writer took some time crafting what he or she thought was a clever message. I guess they get points for originality! Glad you didn't fall for it either!

@bobsongs I got one of the first in our area, it seems…I went to the local Police branch, and they said they had HEARD about them. I posted copies of the three (four?!?) different versions I've received, on my Blog, so folks searching for the wording will know it is a scam.

> **My reply:** Bob, I thought about reporting it, but what can they do? What a great idea about posting the body of the emails! The three I received (from different email addresses) contained the same email body copy. When I googled it, the scam appeared right away.

@macdonellnicola Horrible but loved the dialogue. Warning, idiots, don't mess with us women. We are always smarter than you, even if we don't know how Bitcoin works :-/

> **My reply:** True story! And I seriously don't even know any men who know how to use bitcoin!

CHAPTER 4

REAL-LIFE ENGAGEMENT WRITING

IN THIS CHAPTER:

Handwritten Notes

Engaging Through Email

Engagement for Business

Rewarding Outcomes

Bonus: Engaging Conversations

*"Meaningful connections are not driven by
reciprocity; they're fortified in mutual value."*

— BRIAN SOLIS,
DIGITAL ANTHROPOLOGIST, SPEAKER, AND AUTHOR

When we blog on Instagram, we spend time and energy nurturing online connections. Can you imagine what would happen if we did the same thing in real life?

For thousands of years, letters enabled people who were separated by distance to communicate. Academics began using email in the 1960s, and when the 1970s rolled around, it became a tool for the masses. Do names like CompuServe, AOL, and Yahoo ring a bell? In a relatively short time, we saw widespread acceptance and use of email. I remember working on annual reports for the City of Seattle's Water Department in the 1980s and loved how email paper trails made it easy to "CYA" or "cover your posterior."

Most people are happy to receive a note via snail mail. However, we're at the point in our current culture where the arrival of a handwritten note can almost feel intrusive—like, "Where did you get my address?" Gen X and younger people missed out on this thing called the "phone book," which weighed several pounds and came in handy as a booster seat and toilet paper for the outhouse. It contained names, phone numbers, and addresses of every person publicly listed.

As a graphic designer, I had friends and clients working in the public relations area of marketing. PR people, almost without exception, were hard-wired to acknowledge nearly everything with a handwritten note. Now, even the most hardcore "Miss Manners" rarely does that. Email is faster, and texts are faster still. Terse and instantaneous digital communications can feel inelegant, but they get the job done.

HANDWRITTEN NOTES

In *The Last Lecture,* Professor Randy Pausch gave a great example of how an unexpected outcome can result from a simple gesture, such as writing a thank you note.

A student applied for Pausch's prestigious program at Carnegie Mellon but wasn't chosen. Even so, she sent a handwritten thank you to a staffer who helped set up the interview. The staffer tucked the note into the student's folder, and that was that … until a space unexpectedly became available in the program.

As Pausch went through the files on the other candidates, he discovered the thank you note. There was no calculation on the part of the student, and the staffer who received the note wasn't influential. The simple act of engagement writing made the student stand out. She was offered a coveted opportunity because she took the time to engage (Pausch, Zaslow, 2018).

Handwritten notes are intentional engagement and tokens of esteem. When I was in grade school, my mom made us write thank you notes for Christmas gifts, so I grew up thinking they were expected because it was the proper and polite thing to do. We've become spoiled by technology, but we can still incorporate some of the niceties of handwritten notes into our digital communications.

Some of my Instagram friends shared their opinions about writing thank you notes, and it was encouraging to know there are children who continue to learn this arcane practice. It's not because I believe in torturing kids, but because it raises the level of civility, and as a bonus, having this skill set may prepare them for social interactions later in life.

When someone takes time to compose a resonant message, it makes an impression. The blog *Mental Floss* posted a story on "15 Forgotten Niceties We Should Bring Back." Two of them were thank you cards and letters (Mental Floss, 2016).

It's a pleasant surprise when we receive a real note in the mail. Our postal carrier, David N., sent a warm and gracious thank you card to my husband and me, which made us feel good about showing our appreciation to a wonderful person so worthy of acknowledgment.

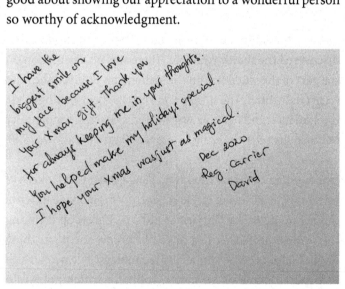

Wouldn't it melt your heart to receive an unexpected note like this one?

ENGAGING THROUGH EMAIL

I have a client whose emails are so curt I sometimes feel as though she's mad about something. Her laser focus on our projects affects the tone and content of her emails, so they feel more like text messages. Elements that convey humanness and regard are omitted. The brevity sometimes feels jarring to me. In discussing this with my sister, she confirmed it has happened to her, too.

Including niceties could help set you apart. It's not difficult to make your communications more engaging. I've found beginning a message with, "Hi, [Name]! I hope you had a great weekend!" works well.

A simple greeting: "Hi, John, how was your weekend?" offers some personal engagement before launching into the reason for the email. Personalization can be effective in our digital communication, yet it's frequently absent. During the pandemic, there were no chance opportunities to meet in the hallway to chat. We missed the small talk that was so important in deepening relationships or transitioning into weighty topics (Methot et al., 2021).

For students, engagement writing establishes positive communications with teachers and other adults in their lives. Text messaging is fast, but sloppy habits can develop and become ingrained. Bad grammar and abbreviations like "TTYL" ("Talk to you later") are widely understood but reinforce habits that can persist into adulthood. Facility with language and the ability to articulate thoughts prepares students for the future. Communication is a valued skill, and cultivating positive interactions are hallmarks of a great team player.

It takes so little time to engage, show interest, regard, and appreciation, and it comes back in spades. Why not do it?

ENGAGEMENT FOR BUSINESS

Each time we communicate with someone, it's an opportunity to establish a connection.

Engagement writing is appropriate with customer support, vendors, suppliers, and others in our business supply chains, including freelancers and service providers. The benefit is a more positive working relationship. And if a problem arises, a call for help might be more positively received.

Customer service agents can be frustrating to deal with at times, and many don't have the clout to make decisions. If a problem is left unresolved, few people will take the time to write a snail mail letter to complain, but when they do, they're hard to ignore. It's essential to be respectful and maintain a tone that invites positive interaction.

Engagement writing can extend to family, friends, coworkers, acquaintances, and anyone we communicate with. When we connect with someone through our writing, we can establish relationships that continue to build over time. When you have a plumbing problem, isn't it nice to know your trusted plumber, Peter, is the person receiving your email?

REWARDING OUTCOMES

Around the country, the 2020–2021 housing market has gone bonkers. Prices are skyrocketing and inventories are at record lows. Even if you have the financial resources to compete, it doesn't always mean you'll succeed. We've all heard of people writing letters to sellers to set themselves apart as the "perfect" buyer for their home. In this example, the homeowner had invested great care in creating an extraordinary home. Friends, Leah and John, recognized the seller would appreciate knowing his efforts would continue to be enjoyed.

I think this home in Lake Forest Park was waiting to find us. We knew it when we first stepped inside. The Japanese influence inside and out really spoke to us. But we had to make a very quick decision, so we could be first in line. We had heard that a personal letter could influence the seller's decision if there were multiple offers. As you'll see in the letter, we really wanted this house. It's perfect for us—huge kitchen, master on the main floor, no more than two stories, move-in-ready, and close to family. We got it all and a bonus view of Lake Washington, which we've been able to really enjoy. — Leah H.

To Jerry & Sharon J.,

My husband John and I would like you to know how much we love your home. We have been looking for the perfect home for us, and we believe we've found it.

We are a couple in our late 60s/early70s, hoping that our next and likely final home will be the perfect one for us. Our two daughters are grown and have moved out, so we are ready to live in a home we've always dreamed of. Lake Forest Park is close to our autistic younger daughter, who lives in a group home in Shoreline.

Years ago, we visited our oldest daughter in Japan, where she was attending school near Kyoto. We fell in love with the culture, architecture, and beautiful gardens that were everywhere. Over the years, we have continued to admire and incorporate an Asian influence in our homes. So, of course, we were happy that your home found us and we're able to make this offer.

We just want you to know that we admire and appreciate what you've done to your home. It's evident that your attention to detail in the custom millwork was done with love and care. The shoji screens are extraordinary. The craftsmanship is just outstanding. Even the colors you chose for each room are special. When touring the house, we were pleased to see the *tansu* chest in the master bedroom. We have two large pieces ourselves, and now we know right where to put one of them. We hope the photos we have included demonstrate to you how much we have embraced the Asian style in our own lives.

Also, we are very appreciative of the landscaping you have done. Again, it was obviously created with much love. We would certainly enjoy resting quietly in many of the beautiful spaces you have created. Thank you for that. At our age, peace and tranquility are very important to our health and happiness.

We hope you will seriously consider our offer. We would take good care of what you have built over the years and hope that you are moving to another home you can grow to love as much as this one.

Warm regards,
John K. & Leah H.

BONUS: ENGAGING CONVERSATIONS

My husband, David, and I have had a house on Airbnb since 2014. We've met some fascinating, fun, and wonderful people. Some have become real-life friends, and we treasure the connections we've made. Here are a few exchanges that resulted from engagement writing on a short-term rental site where communication is usually not engaging.

Cambria

After a recent stay, I received an email message that read:

Good morning,

What a sweet slice of heaven! Thank you for opening your beautiful home to us. We had a wonderful time! We've headed out a little early—just letting you know in case new folks are arriving today.

Be well and thanks again,
Cambria

It was such a surprising and charming note, so I responded with:

Cambria, thank you!

David and I were so glad you were getting some good weather during your stay!

I have a question - did Daisy have fun? I hope so!

Many thanks for the reservation, and best wishes for a safe and happy summer,

Cheers/Terri

It was already a delightful exchange, and I knew if Cambria ever requested another stay in our Airbnb, my response would be a resounding YES! Then I received another email, saying:

Daisy had the very BEST time! Upon arrival, she ran circles around the yard with the biggest dog smile on her face.

I made a little story on my Instagram account - check it out. It is such a dreamy spot; thanks again for sharing!

Best,
Cambria

p.s. I have already ordered my own copy of the cookbook! :)

Cambria discovered a special, vintage cookbook in our Airbnb kitchen, and by telling me about it, I recognized she's a unique person I'd very much enjoy getting to know. We exchanged three messages each and even became Instagram friends. Cambria is on Instagram as @fieldtripsociety.

Wendy

Another exchange with one of our guests extended to a dozen emails, each more rewarding than before. If we'd handled communication in the standard, superficial way, I doubt the following would have unfolded. Following is an excerpt from our exchange:

Hi Terri,

We all enjoyed our stay so much; what a balm for the soul Horsfall House is. It has such a warm heart. And the dogs had so much fun, and I loved your story about letting the kids and the dogs out at the beginning of the driveway!

We hope to come back many times.

I love old houses and doing research on old homes and old families is a hobby/mild obsession. I have found out quite a bit about the Orr family and the history of the house. I spent the better part of two days hunting for clues about what it looked like originally and trying to decipher the when and why of little mysteries. That's how we found the secret room! I also loved discovering the original pipes for the gaslights and a pair of original hinges on the closet door in the downstairs bedroom!

There were a few mysteries I was unable to solve, but I did solve one that really bugged me; I kept wondering why an outhouse would've been built in 1940?!?

One would presume by the quality of the original finishes in the house that the Orr family was not poor, and surely if there wasn't a bathroom when it was first built, they had one added shortly after that. And why would someone carve the date into an outhouse? So, it drove me a little crazy...

But I solved it!

I thought maybe you guys already know the answer to this mystery, but just in case you didn't, I thought you'd want to know.

I discovered that there was a small CCC camp on the property in 1940, working on public projects in the area. There were seven young men stationed there between the ages of 19 and 23.

I imagine that Mrs. Orr wouldn't be too keen on a pack of young men running in and out of her house, thus the 1940 outhouse! I was so excited to learn this; what a great piece of history! And to think most if not all those young men would be off to fight in the war soon. Truly a cool little piece of history!

Anyway, you guys did such an amazing job restoring the house, and I loved the six photographs of the house at different points in her life. They were a great help in understanding her history. She's a grand old country girl!

Hope you're all well

Thanks again,
Wendy

After reading Wendy's email, I immediately replied:

Dear Wendy,

Thank you for this awesome email!

Each night at dinner, we go around the table with whoever is here and take turns talking about the best part of the day. For me, your email was tops! I read it out loud, and David and I both wondered how in the world you found out such great stuff!

David is a history sleuth, too, and had done quite a bit of digging about Mrs. Orr and her family, but your stories are off the chart!

We, too, wondered about the inscription in the outhouse, "build in 1940" [sic].

GOSH, it just makes me want to get together with you!

David will weigh-in, I'm sure, but I just wanted to tell you how much it meant to us to receive your note today. It really made our day!

Thank you so much, Wendy!

((HUGS))
Terri

Most of our guests via Airbnb exchange a few messages, and a few really "get it." The final example is another where a virtual connection evolved to become a real-life friend.

Susan

In this case, we received an inquiry from someone new to the platform. It can be a risk to accept reservations from guests who have no track record. Still, after exchanging some messages and getting a good feeling about Susan and her husband, Joe, through Susan's communication, we were happy to move forward.

Hi Terri,

My husband Joe will be running the Big Foot 200 in August. The race is finishing up in Randle and we're extremely glad we found your listing! It will likely be just him for the duration (although another runner may join him) and possibly on the last night of his stay, my triplet sons and I may join him. Looking forward to hearing back from you.

Hi Susan!

I didn't know about the Big Foot 200! Thanks for telling me about it! Will your husband be flying into the Seattle-Tacoma airport, then renting a car?

I can see you don't have any reviews yet. I'm guessing you just started your Airbnb profile? Everyone has to start somewhere, and I hope to help ensure a positive experience for you as you begin with Airbnb.

I'm going to go ahead and approve the reservation. As the date grows closer, we will need to be in touch to coordinate the keys, answer any questions you might have, etc.

Please feel free to contact me regarding any concerns :)

Welcome to Airbnb!

Hi Terri,

Thanks for the quick response. Joe will likely be flying into Seattle-Tacoma or possibly to Portland (depending on airfares) and then renting a car. I understand the run will be ending at a school in Randle and starting in Marble Mountain. The runners have four days to complete this journey. Crazy if you ask me, but this is Joe's passion. :-)

I just started to use Airbnb this year but have used VBRO in the past. I find there are more options than a traditional hotel and especially when we are a family of five.

I'll keep you posted where Joe will be flying into.

Thanks again.
Susan

Hi Susan.

It sounds like a grueling event! I could hardly believe what I was reading when I googled it. Wow!

It's impressive that you had the presence of mind to book so early. I think our house will be great for you and Joe and your family. (A running mate is fine assuming Joe vouches for him.)

Randle is about midway between Seattle and Portland. Let's stay in touch and nail down details as the date grows closer.

I'm really excited about the race now! How cool is that?

And thanks for letting me know about your experience with VRBO!

Wishing you a great Wednesday!

Once Joe arrived in Seattle and made his way to Randle, WA, we connected directly with him, and the experience led to a post about his incredible endurance race, The Bigfoot 200. The blog post, entitled "Racing Bigfoot in the Shadow of Mt. St. Helens," was published on *The Medium* and one of my WordPress blogs.

"We meet some of the most interesting people when we take the time to connect.

Imagine running a 200+ mile race in four days, over impossible terrain, with only six hours of sleep.

Some of us think our jobs feel like that!

But in fact, this is exactly what Joe Galioto did, along with 58 other athletes who completed the Bigfoot 200, an extreme endurance run that traversed Mount St. Helens in Washington State." (Nakamura, 2015)

Our communication led to a real-life meeting at our little Seattle retail store, Alki Surf Shop, and we've been friends ever since.

Joe Galioto, Terri Nakamura, and David Horsfall at Alki Surf Shop in West Seattle. Selfie by Joe Galioto.

Connections, friendships, and business relationships develop through the practice of engagement writing. Our lives are richer, and amazing things can take place when we are willing to expend energy to connect with others.

CHAPTER 5

RULES OF ENGAGEMENT

———

IN THIS CHAPTER

What an Instagram Blog Post Looks Like

How to Invite Interaction

What an Instagram Comment Looks Like

How to Get More Comments

Surveys

Contests and Giveaways

Lost and Found in Translation

Engagement Tools

Bonus: Post and Engagement

"People love to be recognized and feel that they matter. Recognize them for engaging."

—MARI SMITH, SOCIAL MEDIA AND POWER INFLUENCER

It seems like a no-brainer to respond to a comment when someone leaves one on your blog post, but amazingly, some people don't bother. I've been guilty of that!

Seven years ago, I started social media accounts for my husband's (and my) little store, Alki Surf Shop, in West Seattle. I posted photos on Instagram and included short captions and maybe a few hashtags, but that was it. At the time, I thought having a presence on Instagram was better than nothing. While researching this book, I went back through our Alki Surf Shop posts and discovered sales opportunities that were lost because I didn't always read responses or engage with readers of our posts. You can avoid this mistake.

The "social" in "social media" implies interacting, but in the example, the content was a broadcast rather than an invitation to engage. Sometimes we miss a chance to interact, but with our goal to grow a community on Instagram, we'll be more successful if we participate in the "give and take" of likes and comments. I haven't seen Instagram engagement described as symbiotic, but I've found it to be the case. Followers don't exist to serve us; they interact with us, and without our community's interest and support, Instagram can go quiet, like an unnurtured blog.

WHAT AN INSTAGRAM BLOG POST LOOKS LIKE

At the end of Chapter 3, I talked about two layers of attention on Instagram—the merits of your images and the use of "teasers." Instagram is an image-sharing platform, so your visual content is the first chance you have to catch the attention of people scrolling through their feeds. (The "feed" shows you posts that have been shared by those you follow.)

A visual is a must, and there are many options including photos, videos, graphics, artwork, quotes, and other types of visual content.

The second opportunity we have to engage and draw attention to is in the written post that is shared with the image. The post can be anywhere from a few sentences up to approximately three hundred words in length. Some Instagram bloggers use the image to represent their written post, but I've found the image and the narrative don't necessarily need to be connected.

Two thousand two hundred characters and your imagination are the only limits for your post. You could include:

- An op/ed post
- A stream of consciousness
- A diary entry
- Poetry
- Creative writing (story)
- A rant!

HOW TO INVITE INTERACTION

Starting a conversation in real life often begins with a question. The same is true on Instagram. It makes people feel valued to be asked what they think. Asking for a reader's thoughts, especially on a relatable topic, often draws meaningful comments. You might be thinking: Of course! Even though it's logical, we often forget to encourage feedback by asking a question.

In engagement writing, it's essential to respond to comments made on your content. There are different philosophies about this. If someone leaves an emoji, or a string of them, it doesn't necessarily lead to engagement, but it shows a person has visited your content and has offered a response. But another way to interpret short or nonverbal responses is that the viewer might speak another language and cannot say something you can understand. Some who don't speak your language are undaunted and will leave a comment in *their* native language. It's possible to decipher comments written in other languages, but the processes aren't always easy.

When it comes to writing posts that activate a reader response, here are a few prompts to initiate engagement:

- Ask a question.
- Ask for an opinion — agree or disagree?
- Ask for a solution — what would they do?
- Ask for them to share their experiences — has this happened to you?

Other activities you can do that remind your followers you exist include:

- Like and comment on, or share other people's content.
- "Save" a post to your collection by tapping the little "ribbon" icon on the right below a post.
- Respond to your reader's comments.
- When you respond to a comment and think of another question, ask!

Some Instagram users believe responses to comments are like rewards and should be dispensed only if a comment is deemed worthy. In other words, if the reply isn't substantial enough, it doesn't deserve an answer. I disagree with this approach. Followers of your feed may be shy. It could take several safe, minimally verbal (or nonverbal, such as emoji) exchanges before a person feels comfortable enough to do more than post smiley faces or a thumbs up. Interaction matters, and it nurtures connections. It contributes to growing our connections with others.

Of course, when an account has many thousands, or even millions, of followers, it's not realistic to expect a response to every comment.

According to media monitoring service, Mention:

- 52 percent of Instagram accounts have fewer than 1,000 followers.
- 37 percent have 1,001–10,000 followers (known as "Nano-influencers").
- 8 percent have 10,001 to 100,000 followers (known as "Micro-influencers").
- One-third of one percent (.32 percent) of accounts have more than 100,000 to 1 million+ followers on the platform (known as "Macro-influencers").

Eighty-nine percent (89 percent) of users have the bandwidth (capacity) to respond to comments on a post, but many don't. Those who routinely engage are pretty special!

WHAT AN INSTAGRAM COMMENT LOOKS LIKE

- An emoji or string of emojis
- A simple one or two-word comment. For example: "Brilliant click!" or "Great shot!"
- A response to any prompts you've shared, such as "What do you think?" or "How would you feel … "
- A response written in another language using characters or alphabets you can't decipher.

Besides viewing your followers' content and interacting with it, it's essential that you reply when someone takes the time to leave a comment. When you reply and use the commenter's name, it's even more meaningful. When we see or hear our names, we pay attention. This phenomenon is known as "personalization." Marketers and advertisers use personalization in the emails and direct mail marketing messages we receive every day. One of the reasons these marketing methods have a good return on investment (ROI) is personalization.

Adding the message recipient's name to the subject line of an email, the rate of being opened by the recipient increases by 20 percent (Sahni, Wheeler, and Chintanguta, 2016). Entrepreneur, Syed Balkthi, says, "For most marketers, lack of personalization is the single most common reason their email marketing doesn't work" (Balkthi, 2020). I haven't seen any data that supports this idea, specifically on Instagram. Still, many practices in digital marketing apply across channels, and I've found, through personal experience, that it's effective on Instagram.

Using someone's name when you reply to them makes it a personal communication. Using their name tells the person you took time to learn who they are. I remember exchanging comments with a new follower in Thailand, and she was surprised when I used her name and even wondered how I knew it! My husband always says I'm prescient, but in this case, I clicked on her profile page and saw her name posted there. Personalization has helped me make meaningful connections. It shows the recipient that you go above and beyond.

Reciprocity is part of building connections, but it's not only about liking and commenting on other people's content. Some of the people you follow could include real-life friends who use Instagram for browsing though they've never shared a single post. This type of user is rare but appreciated because they have a personal interest in you and interact with your content.

I know professional photographers in real life who are on Instagram. They're insanely talented and share beautiful images, but it's all crickets if you look at their Instagram engagement. When someone comments on one of their posts, they either ignore them or minimally respond by saying "thanks." They miss the chance to convert that casual viewer into a fan. It reminds me of someone who doesn't like to mingle at a cocktail party and stands mysteriously to the side, waiting for someone to start a conversation with them. In Seattle in the 1980s and into the 2000s, pro photographers were like gods, but Instagram is a great equalizer, and the "I'm too cool and important to interact" attitude can work against you. It can come across as clueless, or worse arrogant, in relation to the social norms of the platform.

So, a question a camera pro might ask is, "Why bother posting on social media?" To which I'd reply, "It's all about likes, brand recognition, and community building."

The number of "likes" a post receives is an important metric and, until 2019 when Instagram began "hiding likes" in some markets, it was a visible way to assess the popularity of a user or post. But what you see isn't always honest. Some users on Instagram (and other platforms) feel better about themselves when they receive a lot of affirmations, even if the likes and comments are purchased or posted by "bots" (a program that automates tasks) or "click farms." Low-paid workers man click farms, often based in developing countries, who like, click, and comment on posts, and help to create the illusion of popularity and engagement (Oli, 2021).

When Instagram began to conceal "likes," the user could still see the number of likes they received, although they were not visible to the public. They remained visible in the US, but when likes were hidden elsewhere, the number of comments became one of the most visible ways to see if someone's post was getting traction. You can learn more about this in Chapter 9.

HOW TO GET MORE COMMENTS
People ask me how they can get more comments on their posts. The most straightforward way to increase engagement is to respond to a comment. There's an option to ♥ "heart" or

"like" a comment, and some users think by adding a "heart" they're engaging. Nope. It might make you feel like you're doing something to engage, but there's a good likelihood your audience won't connect it directly to you.

It takes almost no effort to like a comment, and it takes only slightly more energy to type a few words and add the person's name, so they realize you're specifically responding to them. A personal response also shows you've considered what someone has written, which makes the exchange more meaningful. Another simple action that also draws comments is to like and comment on other people's posts. They see your comment and will often go to your profile and see what you've recently shared.

Blogger, Jon Morrow, breaks down the strategy into a simple formula: Traffic + Engagement + Emotion = Bunches of Comments (Morrow, 2020). But *relevance* is an integral part of the formula. Whether on Instagram or elsewhere, a blogger needs to create engaging content that has intellectual, emotional, or relevant appeal. Ask yourself: will your audience relate?

SURVEYS

Engagement writing is a wonderful way to get to know your readers and a way for them to get to know *you*. Have you ever heard of a "slam" book? It was a popular fad in the 1950s–70s where spiral notebooks full of questions were primarily circulated among teenagers, and each participant could write their answers. Even kids enjoy it when they are asked to share their opinions and thoughts. Using the feature called "Instagram Stories," you can invite your community to participate in a survey or opinion poll.

CONTESTS AND GIVEAWAYS

Besides using relevant hashtags and responding to the comments you receive, HubSpot suggests hosting a contest or giveaway to increase engagement (Bernazzani, 2020). Including a call to action, e.g., "Click the link in my bio to register for the drawing," you provide an exciting and fun way to get your audience interested. There have been times when I've been given sample devices to test or review, and after completing my assignment, I've offered them to anyone who reads to the bottom of my post. All they must do for a chance to "win" is to contact me via DM if they're interested. It's a great way to find a home for a new item you no longer need.

LOST AND FOUND IN TRANSLATION

Instagram is a global "city that never sleeps." No matter what time of the day or night, there is an active community out there viewing, clicking, scrolling, and commenting on the content that comes through their feeds. If you're on the west coast of the US and tend to be nocturnal, you could find yourself with lots of friends and followers in Asia and Europe. They're the ones who are awake and enjoying their morning coffee when it's late-night in Seattle.

English is the most spoken language worldwide in 2021 (Smigiera, 2021). What if English isn't your native language? Some people you meet speak languages other than English and post their content in their native languages. How is it possible to connect with them?

English-speaking countries have relatively low rates of bilingualism, but I've discovered that many people I've met in Japan, Korea, Malaysia, and most of Europe speak English. If someone posts in another language, you can select the "See Translation" link beneath a post or bio to convert the text to English (and vice versa). Does it impede your chances to make friendships with those who don't share your language? Absolutely not. Some who blog on Instagram will post both in their native language and English.

In 2017, Instagram began to offer automatic translations of captions and profiles and currently supports thirty-six languages (Sehl, 2019).

According to Facebook, Instagram comments, captions, and profiles are now translated automatically based on the language they're written in and the language setting of the person viewing it. A user can see translations for posts and profiles, but there isn't an easy way to translate comments from your language to another directly in Instagram. This is problematic, and according to the bonus post at the end of the chapter, users would appreciate real-time translation. Multiple language translation has been available on Facebook for a long time, but as of May 2021, it hasn't surfaced on Instagram.

To circumvent this problem, I sometimes look at a post through my Google Pixel's "Translate" built-in camera feature, which allows me to decipher a foreign language and create a response. There are also apps, both on iOS and Android, and online tools where users can translate posts and comments.

ENGAGEMENT TOOLS

Social media dashboards are tools that help you manage your social media accounts across different channels, such as Instagram, Twitter, Facebook, LinkedIn, and Pinterest.

They monitor likes, shares, and other engagement and make it possible for you to easily schedule content and measure the effectiveness of what you post. I found a list on Investopedia that struck me as pretty solid. I've excerpted a few I've used personally or have been used and recommended by people I know. The list below shows free or inexpensive options, but each tool offers more costly plans with greater functionality. The prices are current as of June 2021.

- **Sprout Social** is considered a great overall tool. At the most basic level ($99/month), the dashboard can be used to monitor five profiles, schedule, publish, and access customer relationship tools, among other features. It includes social listening (where you learn if your brand has been mentioned and detect if the sentiment is positive, negative, or neutral).

- **Hootsuite.** At its most basic level ($49/month), a single user can monitor ten social accounts, schedule unlimited posts, and access messages across accounts in one mailbox. Users can access a quick snapshot for insights about fans and followers.

- **Buffer.** The free version is … free and allows a single user three social channels and ten scheduled posts. The Pro Plan ($15/month) allows a single user eight social accounts and one hundred scheduled posts per channel. It also enables the creation of a custom schedule, location tagging, and a useful and time-saving engagement feature.

- **SocialPilot.** This app is recommended for small teams. At the basic level ($50/month), it allows bulk scheduling and reporting across twenty-five social profiles, and real-time social engagement at half the price of some of its competitors (Johnson, 2021).

I'm a small fry and mainly focus on engagement, so I use the Pro version of Buffer. In 2020, Buffer added an engagement feature to the Pro version that blew my socks off. It gives me a bird's-eye view of my posts, including the number of comments on each, detects "sentiment," and highlights comments that are waiting for responses. I can respond directly in Buffer, which dramatically reduced the time I spend answering comments.

When there are lots of short comments, Buffer advises that it's not necessary to respond to every comment. However, when you're starting out, I encourage you to acknowledge every comment left by your audience members. (It's worth mentioning that I am not sponsored by Buffer, but their service is just *that* good!)

BONUS: POST AND ENGAGEMENT

Another example where the image has nothing to do with the blog post featured a picture of one of my cats, whose face was reflected in a mirror. It received 1,140 likes and gathered 333 comments. The number of comments is the total number, including my replies. Among the comments are some beneficial features that Instagram should implement! Instagram, are you reading this? Go to the post and check out what your users want!

If you could ask I.G. for a feature, what would it be? Even though it seems lately I see more of my favorite people, I was thinking about this recently. I have a wish list. Can you add to it?

HERE ARE SOME IDEAS:

A global setting to always see captions translated to one's native language. Is it possible to do the same with replies? Currently, I use Google translate and then do a reverse translation to write a response. It takes time, and I can't always do it.

Could we see more photos posted by people who are on our favorites list rather than those chosen by the algorithm? I make special trips to visit pages of those I like but sometimes never see. In the old days, we would simply see real-time photos posted by anyone we follow. Could this be an option?

Could Instagram post an ad that includes basic rules of play? Some people don't know that it's not okay to use apps or buy followers, and other people don't know it's not okay to like bomb or comment bomb or use automation. They land in the I.G. time-out corner and are told they've violated a rule. A periodic reminder would be great!

When a user has a private account, others can't see samples of the kinds of photos in that feed. Could I.G. mention to private accounts there's a reduced likelihood of being followed if others can't view their contents?

And could Instagram build a verification requirement to reduce the volume of new fake accounts?

FINAL WISH ITEM: is there any way the public hashtagged contents on Instagram could be made accessible by external search?

Maybe these things are too picky! What do you think?

I would love to know if there is anything on your wish list?

Wishing you a safe and wonderful weekend!

And for those who celebrate, happy #Caturday!

Photos: #catshenanigans and an in-progress #quarantine #kitchen #remodel. #cats #catsofinstagram #catstagram #catlovers #instacat #instakitty #sillyanimals #petstagram #mirror #cathelper #lockdown #kitchenproject #frenchdoors #transomwindow #potrack #seattle #centraldistrict #madrona

Following are some great examples of engagement in response to my post. It was really cool to see some of the ideas. As a writer, when you engage with your audience, it builds connectedness. For companies, it also leads to greater loyalty and customer satisfaction. The replies made me wish there was a way to convey some of the suggestions to Instagram.

@webgrrrl I agree wholeheartedly about wishing photos posted and stayed in real-time order—as a user option, that would be fantastic! My biggest quibble with the game rules is that I.G. all but holds a gun to our heads to use hashtags…but they're utterly pointless for private users, since nobody but people already following them can see their posts in a hash feed. I think an option to allow private users to set a limited preview for potential users might be very useful for them: I know tons of people refuse outright to follow private accounts. Would it be cool if I.G. instituted a "suggestion box" for noodges like us?

@gfridell_photo I agree Instagram should change. It should show everyone you follow and sort it in chronological order from when the photo was posted and remember where you stopped so you don't have to scroll through a lot to get to where you were last time.

@jaf5786 I would agree about the caption translation. I also try to use google translate, but it is time consuming. The auto-translation can be quite baffling to understand! Another good idea (as you mention) would be to prioritize photos/posts of those accounts I follow who I have the most interaction with. (Note from Terri: Instagram has attempted to show posts of people with whom you engage. @staticulator and I did an experiment. We weren't seeing each other's posts. So we went through and liked a bunch of photos on each other's feeds and made comments. Bingo. Our photos began to show up.)

@sc_syd Your thoughts are very precise. I agree with a lot of them in the list. I don't know how the order appearing on my feed is decided, but it seems I miss a lot of photos. Recently one person following each other a long time unfollowed me. I realized I hadn't seen his photos in a long time. Not intentionally, but they didn't come up on my feed. Anyway, I unfollowed him. It's just my rule. And I think one third of the photos on my feed are advertisements. It makes it much harder to check through actual following people. Oh, one more thing I really wish. If a person posts so frequently or dozens of posts at a time, just show one of the photos within 12 hours or so. Do you understand what I mean? Flickr's platform can choose like that.

@mrron9 On my wish list: I'd love a hashtag translator.

@subegardie …posting lots of photos the same day is boring, time consuming and one has less time to appreciate other pictures. One thing I hate is having fake followers that obviously start following to chat and although you eliminate [them] the D.M. stay as followers.

@turinepi I wish I could see the posts of all the accounts I follow like in the past. It was sooo nice. (Note from Terri: Originally, Instagram users would log on, and all posts shared by people a user followed would be posted in chronological order. Instagram's algorithm currently only shows content it "thinks" a user will like.)

@chinneo.lhungdim Terri, I would also want that language translation feature. I find people who follow/comment on mine, and when I go to their feed, I cannot understand what they have written in their language…and as a result, not able to comment on their photos for fear of writing something totally different…

@Carolmiles2018 As regards Instagram you're definitely not being picky as your ideas make complete sense….Especially the translation of captions, etc., and the controlling of fake accounts… It's so frustrating to have to block so many each day for them to pop up again under a new username but often with the same profile pic…And I hardly ever follow a private account now because like you say it's important to be able to view their content.

@k.n.o.w.n. My one I.G. hope is to fast forward videos. I would get to see more content that way.

CHAPTER 6

INSTAGRAM AS A DIGITAL DIARY

IN THIS CHAPTER:

Instagram Diaries Connect Us with Others

The Written Part of Your Diary

Prompts to Get You Thinking

Instagram as an Art Journal

Public versus Private

The Visual Part of Your Diary

A Few Photography Tips

BONUS: How I Journal on Instagram

"The best time to begin keeping a journal
is whenever you decide to."

—HANNAH HINCHMAN, AUTHOR

———————

D o you remember what you were doing in February 2016? Most people can't, but by keeping a digital diary on Instagram, you have a repository of experiences you can find with a quick scroll through your feed. Instagram is a great place to share your thoughts about the happenings in your life, it's easy to share with friends and family, and it's used frequently in that way.

Although there are a bunch of ways people blog on Instagram, I'm going to do a dive into diaries or journals because it's something a lot of people will find familiar. If you're intrigued about the idea of blogging on Instagram but you don't have a specific writing objective, a journal-style approach might work for you.

I bet some of you have tried keeping a diary at some point. The word "diary" is understood as a daily entry, but the commitment doesn't need to be rigid. No matter the frequency, it's still a capture of that day. Many people resolve to start a diary at the beginning of January. By the time they get to January 15, they say, "Screw it." When a task feels like a chore, it's a negative reinforcer. Besides, is anyone keeping track?

When I was a student in 2019, taking an expository writing class, I kept a journal each day for ten weeks. The assignment sounded fun—like a flashback to the tenth grade. I looked forward to it but also dreaded it because, on many days, nothing noteworthy happened. I didn't want to write about an uneventful day, but if we're being honest, some days are dull.

The difference between my journal assignment and other diaries I began and abandoned over the years was that I would have an audience of at least one person—the professor. The idea that I was writing something that I knew would be read affected the way I wrote about each day. I didn't want the professor to know my life was actually pretty boring, so I challenged myself to find ways to make it interesting.

I was forced to maintain a journal because it was part of a class, but for the average person, what compels us to keep a diary in the first place? They're hard to maintain and add one more thing to do in an already busy life. If you miss a day and feel guilty about it, you might go back through your calendar and texts, trying to re-create whatever happened, but you feel like you're cheating. Maybe it's tempting to get a bit creative and rewrite history *just a little* because you wish things on a given day had turned out differently. After all, you are primarily writing it for yourself, right? Reading through it in the future, maybe you'll review your diary entry for that day and remember it exactly the way you've written it.

In 2007, author Louis Menand published an essay in the *New Yorker* about why we read diaries. He wrote:

> "Diarizing is a natural, healthy thing, a sign of vigor and purpose, a statement, about life, that we care, and that non-diarizing or, worse, failed diarizing is a confession of moral inertia, an acknowledgment, even, of the ultimate pointlessness of one's being in the world."

Ouch.

Menand goes on to describe motivation and theories about keeping a diary. For example, it's difficult for most people to keep a journal going because it's hard to believe their entries are worthwhile simply because they recount something that happened to *them*. If you're recording your entries for posterity, you might think no one would be interested in reading it, including *you*. But it doesn't have to be that way!

Instagram as a diary is a more inviting experience because you can express your creativity in addition to sharing your thoughts. You'll find it's portable, convenient, and easy to use. By using Instagram as a diary, photos become the spark for recalling what you're thinking about on a given day. And if you have readers, you're motivated to find the moments you most want to share and remember. Win-win!

INSTAGRAM DIARIES CONNECT US WITH OTHERS
Through engagement with others, we feel more connected and less alone.

Journaling for Mental Health asserts that journaling can help improve our feelings of mental well-being by reducing stress and helping us manage anxiety and depression. In combination with other activities that contribute to a healthy lifestyle, a journal can help us figure out what's causing our stresses and give us opportunities for "positive self-talk." (URMC, ND) It has also been found that journaling can be a cathartic experience because putting your thoughts in writing helps you process them (Cassata, 2021). In addition, a community on Instagram expands your social circles and may be a way to deal with feelings of loneliness.

Share more. Feel better.

THE WRITTEN PART OF YOUR DIARY: PROMPTS TO GET YOU THINKING

A digital journal can begin with a simple idea. We have a family tradition at our house: no matter who is with us at dinnertime, we take turns going around the table, with each person sharing the "best part of their day." The saying goes: "Even on a crummy day, there's a best part." If you think about your days that way, you begin to see tiny jewels that are often overlooked. It can be that easy.

You can consider using Instagram as a gratitude journal to remind yourself of the good people and things in your life. You're writing for yourself, but your community is invited to read your musings and respond to them. You might inspire others to think more appreciatively about their own lives.

In Chapter 8 you'll learn about the mechanics of creating a blog post for Instagram. But if you're wondering how you might use Instagram as a diary, Margarita Tartakovsky, MS associate editor of Psych Central, has written an article listing thirty writing prompts designed to get to know yourself better. Some have been adapted here as possible themes or content ideas for your Instagram feed.

- What was the best part of your day?
- What advice would you give to your younger self?
- What are some of your most unforgettable moments?
- What makes you smile?
- What do you most value in your life?
- The kindest things to do for yourself
- Who are the people who matter most and why?
- What do you wish others knew about you?
- What makes your life complete?
- Have you shown compassion recently? With whom and how?
- What do you love most about your life?
- What brings tears to your eyes?
- Who or what was your first love?
- Describe yourself in ten words
- What question do you urgently need answered?
- What inspires you?
- What makes you happiest? (Tartakovsky, 2014)

By starting with a prompt, you can write with a purpose. You'll begin thinking intentionally about daily occurrences, what matters most to you, and experiences to share with others.

"Journaling helps us figure out who we are, what we need and what we want. It can help us make better decisions and focus on the very things that support us in taking compassionate care of ourselves and others."

— MARGARITA TARTAKOVSKY, M.S.

INSTAGRAM AS AN ART JOURNAL

Instagram diaries are digital versions of art journals used by artists who collect thoughts, ideas, and other materials that can be used to inspire or remember. The analog versions could be sketchbooks or multimedia and dimensional—with pressed leaves or other objects, along with words as art, and more. Author David Sedaris published a visual diary that was more of an art book than what we imagine when we think of art journals. Still, I think the main difference with visual diaries is that they work best for people who want an accessible place to document their creations.

Visual diaries have been around for a long time. One of the most famous visual journals was Leonardo da Vinci's. He created fifty volumes over the course of thirty years that included his writing, sketches, and ideas, which he began in the early 1480s at the age of twenty-six until he was sixty-seven years old (Hdez, 2014).

Instagram is a fantastic outlet to show your creativity both with writing and with visual content. Just like analog journals and diaries, Instagram allows writers to express themselves through words and images.

But in addition to this, it has the potential to be used for marketing. Suppose you're a ceramics artist, create works of handblown glass, or otherwise have an Etsy store or an online business. In that case, Instagram lets you show potential customers what you do and gives you the chance to connect and communicate with interested people.

An image can evoke a memory, just as any narrative you include can help re-create a moment. You can add more than a short description and a few hashtags to identify what's in an image. As an Instagram blogger, you have an opportunity to document your life and/or the process you followed to create your work. This might even remind you of the steps you took that resulted in a new technique.

PUBLIC VERSUS PRIVATE

If your account is public, there is a chance that whatever you write will be read by someone. People who read your words might empathize or relate and feel the need to say something. Knowing there's a likelihood of having an audience is one of the main elements that sets Instagram apart from a traditional diary.

If you're apprehensive about having a public diary, you have an option to make your Instagram diary private. It still offers a place to keep your photos and posts, and you'll always have the option to make it public. I've seen users who privatize their accounts and others who start with a private account and make it public. If you have a public profile and have followers, they will continue to see your posts even if you make your account private. Also, public accounts can be found on the Internet when the account name is entered in a search.

In thinking about the pros and cons of making your account public or private, the decision depends on your goals. If you would like Instagram to function as a private diary, your account should be closed to followers. It's still possible to have an audience, much like in the way your Facebook is available only to those you allow to see it. But if you would like the chance to experience interaction with people, having an account available to those interested in your niche, topics, profile, or interests will open the possibility of a larger audience. Another benefit of posting publicly: Instagram is a social media channel. Note the word "social." The interaction with others on the platform is one of the most gratifying things about being there.

A valuable benefit of choosing a public account is that it makes it easier to grow your audience. The average Instagram user will not pursue or follow a person with a private account. A visual diary is an ideal solution for artists. Jewelry designers, craftspeople, weavers, painters, and performers have a worldwide stage to show work and tell the stories behind it. Most of us look at journaling as a place to store our thoughts but it's also an opportunity to acquire an audience that is interested in what we create.

THE VISUAL PART OF YOUR DIARY

The idea of using Instagram as a place to blog your diary might seem daunting. Instagram is a visual channel, and some users feel uneasy about their ability to create captivating images to go with their written narratives.

There are solutions to this dilemma. There are likely many bloggers who are not necessarily artistically talented. They use image sources to find photos or illustrations that go with their blog posts. You can do the same here. You'll find information in Chapter 12 about image resources that offer stunning photos that are available to use in your posts at no charge.

Do you lack confidence and doubt your photos are "good enough" to share publicly? Even if you are doubtful, I would encourage you to try. I've noticed that without fail if you are a crummy or mediocre photographer and you continue to post on Instagram, you will become a better photographer over time. Using the platform, you will see many examples of photos and styles you like, and you'll begin to think more about the way you take pictures. As you become more comfortable on the platform, you'll feel empowered to experiment, and over time, your photos will evolve, and you'll start feeling like you're a pretty good photographer. And guess what? Other people will think so, too.

Having spent decades of my life working with professional photographers as I directed photo shoots, through trial and error, I discovered ways to take better photos.

When a commercial photographer shoots an assignment, it's not unusual for them to shoot dozens or even hundreds of exposures. By shooting a lot of options, it increases the chances of getting one excellent shot.

A FEW PHOTOGRAPHY TIPS

There is a section of photography tips in Chapter 9 that offers advice and applications that can help you improve the quality of the photos you share. You'll also find other resources for sharing or editing images. Here are a few basic tips:

- Shoot pictures that are in focus.

- Use available light when possible.

- Think about framing a shot, so the most important part is the focus. For example, avoid shooting a photo of a person standing in front of a tree. It could look like the tree is growing out of the top of their head!

Don't be intimidated, because it's easier than you think. And the advice you read is meant to help—not stop you from jumping onto Instagram to share your writing and point of view. The main thing is to get out of the starting gate. I've posted seventeen thousand photos in the past ten years. My first photo was a picture of my cat. It wasn't great, and I didn't know what I was doing. Don't worry if you've only shot photos of your family or vacation pictures. In fact, don't let anything get in your way. Whatever you choose to do will be a perfect way to start your Instagram diary.

BONUS: HOW I JOURNAL ON INSTAGRAM, BY MARION DRIVER, INSTAGRAM BLOGGER

Marion Driver (@mariondriver) has been on Instagram since May of 2015. She's a micro-influencer with more than 1,100 followers. I asked her a few questions about her experiences blogging on Instagram.

How long have you been writing long-format captions on Instagram?

I've been on Instagram for about six years and have been writing long captions for about half that time. When I started writing, I found it was very therapeutic for me—very calming and soothing.

Do you ever look at Instagram as a diary?

That's how I think of my posts here. Reflecting a bit, it has indeed become a diary or journal. I see photos I've posted of my family, record my stories, and I can look back and remember the moment.

Have longer captions increased your audience engagement?

Yes, but the caption needs to be really good. Sometimes when you put things out there, it provokes people into participation, which isn't a bad thing. I can compose on my phone, but if I'm trying to work something out and I need to see it in a broader space, I'll put it on paper first. I feel like I do have something to say; I have a story—many stories—to tell and I use Instagram to share them.

CHAPTER 7

WHY BLOG ON INSTAGRAM?

———

IN THIS CHAPTER:

Motives for Blogging on Instagram

Advantages of Blogging on Instagram

Ways Blogging on Instagram Helps Us

Limitations

SEO and Search

BONUS: Why I Blog on Instagram

"Writing is thinking out loud. Blogging is thinking out loud where other folks think back."

—LIZ STRAUSS, FRIEND AND MARKETING THOUGHT LEADER

Disruption is what happens when goods and services get stuck and an innovation comes along that provides new value. No one imagined how Uber would disrupt transportation or how Airbnb would disrupt the hotel business. Blogging on Instagram is a small but disruptive idea that takes a social media platform designed to share photos and uses it as a place to write.

For forty years I was a professional graphic designer. I was given words that were written by advertising copywriters, editorial and technical writers, corporate writers, and authors, and charged with incorporating their words into design projects, whether it was a book, magazine, or annual report. My goal was to make words beautiful and readable. I'd read the text of each and every project—all the words—because I knew it was important and could inform design. Not all designers do that!

For me, blogging was an inevitable activity. My husband is an ad guy and I aspired to write too, so I started my first blog in 2005. I practically had to beg friends and family to visit my blog, but when someone read my posts and replied, I loved it!

When Instagram came along in October 2010, I was intrigued by the idea of image sharing and joined in April 2011. As a designer who had art-directed hundreds of photoshoots, I was always the one standing behind the professional photographers who were shooting the photos. Just as blogging gave me a place to write, Instagram gave me a place to share the photos I took.

I'd been on Instagram for seven years when I left my job in 2018. I was in a state of uncertainty, and frankly, I felt nauseous. Instagram proved to be a social media life preserver. I remember the post on my final day at work. It was raining, and a close friend was there with me. I was certain it was the right thing to do but still felt unsettled. My mind raced about the changes I was going through professionally, and Instagram became the repository of my thoughts.

I shared on Instagram without any expectations—I just put my angst "out there." Once I started writing extended captions, people who followed my feed became supporters in my journey. Besides the therapeutic value, I became better acquainted with my community through our exchanges. My experience shows there may be friends out there we don't even know about, and importantly, we're not alone. When these interactions began to happen on my Instagram feed, I started to get to know long-time social media friends whom I'd previously known only superficially. The seeds of real friendships were planted through our conversations.

Up until my career change, Instagram was my visual diary. I posted daily images with hashtags, and if I added a description, it was hastily written. Most captions on Instagram continue to fall into this format, and that's OK! Sometimes when there are just a few words to read it lets people scroll through the content feed more quickly. At that time, my account was moderately successful. I had fewer than three thousand followers, but as my engagement grew, more followers saw my posts and I began expanding my community.

Research on influencer behaviors conducted by Fohr and Later both revealed longer Instagram captions to be in the spotlight and get better engagement (Canning, 2020). I inadvertently discovered this firsthand as I worked through my career change.

MOTIVES FOR BLOGGING ON INSTAGRAM

If you write for personal enjoyment or if you're a professional blogger who hungers for an audience and engagement, you might be surprised to find a satisfying experience awaits you on Instagram. There are differences between writing for pure joy versus blogging strategically. Pro bloggers generally adhere to a posting schedule and write to incorporate repetitive keyword phrases to increase a post's visibility through search. Since I liked writing for "fun," these contrivances always felt unnatural to me. I learned how to build and manage WordPress sites when I returned to college, and I learned the importance of SEO (search engine optimization). I'd run my post through Yoast (a popular WordPress plugin tool that helps people optimize their posts) and discover I needed to shorten paragraphs, insert subheads, and repeat search terms in particular places to get to an acceptable score. At the end of the process, my writing felt stilted.

When your goal is to write for personal enjoyment, SEO constraints can feel stifling (Chapter 9, which focuses on Instagram blogging mechanics, outlines the process in more detail). And although pro bloggers might find it strange to blog on Instagram without integrating SEO, it can be equally effective. Blogging on Instagram offers us the power to convert readers to take the next step, perhaps even more compellingly than if they landed on a blog post through search. Your relationships with your readers make them more inclined to believe you and follow your recommended actions. The ability to drive conversions is the special sauce that makes Instagram a great blogging platform.

When you blog on Instagram, you can accomplish several objectives. Among them:

- You have a place to write and share your thoughts using long-narrative captions.
- You can share photos and use captions to deliver information that relates to them.
- You give your followers a chance to engage with you and get to know you.
- You can build a sense of place in a global community with people you come to recognize as part of your online neighborhood.
- You can crowdsource opinions or conduct informal polls or research.
- You can easily access and view an archive of your words and images.

Your posts appear in reverse chronological order and the time stamps make it easy to reference where you were in your thoughts at a specific point in your history.

By 2020, Growth Badger reported there were 600 million blogs worldwide (Byers, 2021). Considering the average blog length is 2,100 to 2,400 words, Instagram's current limit of about 300 words plus hashtags might feel more like a recap than a blogpost. But you can say a lot in 300 words! For a blogger, maybe the word length constraint feels like being a black Labrador in a yard with an invisible fence and bracing for the shock of going over the line. But by writing a post of 300 words or less, you learn to decide what's important. If you have a blog property, you can write fully fleshed-out extended posts that live there as the entrée and use your Instagram post as the hors d'oeuvre. If your followers on Instagram like what they're reading or are interested in learning more, there's a good chance they'll investigate your blog. You can suggest your readers click your profile link for more information, and many will. Instagram can be a springboard to cultivate more connections and introduce more people to your blog.

It's not very gratifying when a writer does all the work needed to publish a new blog post and receives limited or no feedback. It can feel like speaking into an empty auditorium! I used to begin writing letters to people and not finish or mail them. A friend told me I was writing the letters to myself. I think bloggers who write on blogs where they receive no engagement might also feel they are writing to themselves, which isn't *necessarily* bad. Sometimes we feel better when we get thoughts out of our heads and in a form we can see.

It takes a lot of work to develop content and to cultivate a following on a blog. Many bloggers practice reciprocal liking, following and commenting, and promoting their content via email and social media. There are similarities with Instagram except there isn't a need to promote content outside of the app. Instead, you remain on Instagram when participating in reciprocal activities.

A personal diary may be an exception when it comes to an audience. When making a commitment to journaling, after earlier abandoned attempts, there's a potential to shirk then chalk it up as a failed new year's resolution. We tend to think of diaries as something that no one will read. Still, every writer, including diarists, writes hoping that his or her words outlast them and will be saved for posterity.

You've heard the phrase, "Get outside," but in making a case for blogging and journaling on Instagram, how about "Get outside of your own head?" Whether you're new to writing, are a casual blogger, or blog professionally, Instagram offers you access to the audience traction and the fulfilling experience of interacting and "getting outside" with your readers.

ADVANTAGES OF BLOGGING ON INSTAGRAM

Writing adds value to sharing on Instagram. When storytelling is part of your post, you have the power to do more than share a nice photo. Instagram has gone from a tool bloggers use to promote their blogs to an intentional destination for Instagram bloggers. I see Instagram bloggers as a new type of influencer.

In 2020, I shared a sponsored Instagram post that drew more than 1,000 likes and 200 comments, and 15 people clicked the link to get more information. I'd never come close to achieving that level of engagement on a blog post.

Blogging on Instagram means you have a presence where your readers LIVE. It takes minutes instead of months to set up your account, so you can start blogging right away. As a casual blogger for 16 years, I've experienced the difference between instant and meaningful feedback on Instagram and waiting for responses on a blog. That part of the Instagram blogging experience makes it an exciting place to write.

Instagram bloggers I've met enjoy publishing their writing, but like most general users, they're also there to see interesting and beautiful content, develop relationships, and experience interaction with people. Except for straight-up influencer accounts, most people aren't selling anything or hoping for you to do anything more than look or comment.

On Instagram, you're not obligated to adhere to a publishing schedule. The Instagram algorithm has traditionally rewarded frequency, and it's still practiced, but in December 2019, Later reported a reduced posting frequency, attributing it to the time and effort required to create quality content (Canning, 2020). In other words, in the past, there was a strong incentive to post every day, but I've noticed, even among my followers, a trend to post when there is something worth sharing.

Your Instagram posts don't wait to be discovered by a web crawler. Your readers don't have to visit your site because your posts are *delivered to them*. Like a blog, you need followers, but you don't need subscribers. And let's not forget how easy it is to jump-start your Instagram audience by inviting Facebook friends and those in your contacts list. There is more about building your community in Chapter 14.

Building a subscribers list takes time and subscribers aren't guaranteed to open your blog post email notification. I found it a bit humiliating to spend time writing, editing, and gathering art for a blog post, then see very few (if any) of my subscribers read or comment. It would have been easier and maybe more satisfying to write a story and email it to a dozen friends!

On Instagram, as in real life, communication is a two-way street. A bond forms with followers on every platform, and many of your Instagram connections who start as strangers will become your friends. I compared friends on Twitter to talking with your neighbors over the digital backyard fence, but Twitter has become noisy, and conversation threads are often too confusing to follow. If you blog on Instagram and invite feedback, your words will be read and responded to—just as it would happen with a real-life friend.

BLOGGING ON INSTAGRAM HELPS US

Studies have shown that writing can be restorative. Courtney E. Ackerman, MSc., says writing therapy is helpful for personal growth (Ackerman, 2021). Also known as journal therapy, it is practiced by individuals or groups, supervised by a psychotherapist. Writing on Instagram can be therapeutic as it helps users improve their outlook and mental health.

M. Cecil Smith, PhD, addressed the question, "What advantages does writing afford to individuals, and how does it impact emotional well-being and cognitive abilities?" Writing about personal events improves your recall and cognitive skills. As you blog on Instagram, you may not immediately see how the writing process itself can make you feel good, but the more you write, the more your reflective thinking and organizational thinking improves. When you write, you can feel more positive, improve your skills, and improve your memory all at the same time (Smith, n.d.).

Another benefit of blogging on Instagram is having something in common with the people we meet. We share a common interest in photography and social media and understand the conventions of participating. Friendships help combat isolation, and this benefit was especially important during 2020. We stayed in touch with virtual friends and felt part of their lives as they felt part of ours. We could share our worries as we all went through the pandemic together.

There are aspects of belonging to a community that feel very much like real life. When a friend hasn't "seen" you for a while, it's not unusual to have them "drop by" your profile to see what you've been up to.

As I wrote longer captions, my words elicited more reactions and opinions from other people. It reminded me of when I began blogging in 2005. Anytime someone commented on one of my blog posts, it was like a gift. It was the same way on Instagram, only better because the comments appeared instantly.

Another surprising benefit of blogging on Instagram is the crossover of friendships from virtual to real life. Virtual friendships are based on the social media interactions we have. Over time, I think it's difficult to sustain a phony persona, and that's a good thing. Because of Instagram, I've met Instagram friends in real life when traveling in Italy, Germany, and in different parts of the US. In every instance where I've met a social media connection in real life, it has been a satisfying and seamless experience. Conversations exchanged on Instagram continue naturally when you're face-to-face. It's great to hear someone's voice, see them smile, and observe their body language. At least for me, my real-life connections have been authentic, and consistent with what I've imagined them to be.

LIMITATIONS

There is a 300-word limit on Instagram posts, and it's currently not possible to insert functional links within the body of the post. Most blog posts contain links that will offer a reader a chance to jump to more information that is often found in another blog post or sometimes on an external site. As of mid-2021, it's not possible to insert clickable links in the text of a post. Some users will insert a "short link." Link shorteners reduce the length of a standard link to roughly fourteen or fifteen characters that make it possible to type it into a browser or copy and paste, but these options are not ideal. But there is a work-around: at least a half dozen bio-link tools enable users to post a single link that will lead to multiple links. LinkTr.ee and Linkin.bio are two that were mentioned earlier in the book.

SEO, or search engine optimization, can't be used in the traditional sense on Instagram. People can find your public Instagram profile through search engines, but they won't find your individual posts. Social media channels tweak features on an ongoing basis, so it could happen in the future. Instagram introduced the ability to add "alt text" to images (which lets vision-impaired visitors understand what is being presented on the screen). By adding alt text, you can provide a customized description of your images. The alt text is searchable within Instagram.

In an Instagram post, tags and mentions function similarly to backlinks as they increase opportunities to have your content seen and discovered (Chacon, 2020). Backlinks, which help SEO by linking one domain to another, are not available on Instagram. As of June 2021, Instagram has been testing a feature to enable external links for all users, but it remains to be seen if and when they will be made available (Ion, 2021).

Another drawback—It isn't possible to collect Instagram data the same way as on a blog. Blog URLs can use Google Analytics to track traffic to the post, including where the readers access the link to a blog post. It's possible to drill into granular information about your readers, how long they stay on a page and links they click, where they go next, and it's even possible to see what kinds of devices they use, and the operating systems on the devices.

More than a billion people use Instagram and its internal search engine, which offers unlimited opportunities to be discovered. You and your content can be found within the platform through the use of username, hashtag and word searches. Hashtags work similarly to keywords on a blog. The search function is convenient and efficient. It's currently not possible to search hashtagged Instagram content on Google. But just as a blog can be discovered randomly using a search engine, so can your content be discovered by Instagram's search engine and its one billion users.

SEO AND SEARCH

I mentioned that having an independent blog comes with the pressure to write frequently and stay on a posting schedule. On top of maintaining a plan, you need to make sure that you adhere to the conventions that allow your blog to be found. I've mentioned that keywords and SEO are automatic expectations. Adding links to external sources and internal pillar content is important if you're serious about blogging and want your content to be discovered through organic search. Organic search results are not *paid*. They are the top results of typing terms into a search engine and seeing what shows up in the search engine results pages (SERP).

On Instagram, the average user has limited awareness of how people find their content or how many have encountered it. They can see how many comments they received and how many people liked a post. In 2019, in some countries, Instagram hid the number of likes, making them visible only to the original poster. Instagram believed hiding likes would be good for mental health.

Some users welcomed the chance to experiment away from their core content without being visibly penalized. Remember, Instagram categorizes users according to what they share and what they like, so once you venture outside of your content niche, your visibility and engagement will likely drop.

Individual users can see basic increased or decreased likes and comments, but if you have a business account, you can access more insights about where your engagement is coming from and what actions visitors take. In the US in May 2021, Instagram rolled out the optional hiding of likes with the idea that content creators could share without concern about the number of likes (Perez, 2021).

According to inbound marketing company Hubspot:

> "... Instagram has officially reached more than one *billion* active monthly users -- which means it's now more popular than social media giants such as Twitter or LinkedIn.

That's a lot of users sitting around, waiting to see your content. So, how can you reach all of those users and create opportunities for them to engage with your brand?

The answer might surprise you—SEO for Instagram."

Is it *really* possible to employ the same SEO techniques used on web pages within a social media app?

According to Hubspot, it is. They say the trick isn't shoe-horning Instagram into your existing SEO strategy, but rather using what you know about SEO to drive organic growth to your Instagram account. Instagram has built-in search functions that act like a mini-Google perusing its user base. Think of Instagram as having its own search engine (Pope, 2019).

Marketing consultant, Matt Carracino, says, "Hashtags on Instagram function in a similar way to keywords that help SEO on blogs, websites, paid advertising, and other social media platforms. On Instagram, hashtags should be researched prior to use to check up on competitors, ensure clean content, and align with the blogger's goals." He notes that since your Instagram bio may be found when searched on the web, it's essential to pay attention and make sure it contains the most important information about your account, including a few keywords.

Just as users may welcome the chance to try out new content types without fear of losing "likes," writers can use Instagram for the personal satisfaction of writing and engaging, without the demands of a blog. If you *are* a blogger trying to build traffic to your business, you will find great access to an audience where you can build awareness of your brand and cultivate engagement using Instagram as a springboard.

Using a popular social media channel in an unexpected way benefits users as well as the platform itself, because when more people are drawn to the channel, everyone wins. Blogging on Instagram gives you a broader audience than you would probably experience on a blog you own. You can enjoy a greater readership and get more engagement, and that kind of exposure and engagement is rewarding.

I spoke with Sarah Bauer, Instagram blogger and friend, about the evolution of lengthening posts and using Instagram as a blog. You'll find examples of increasing engagement in the bonus content that follows.

BONUS: SARAH BAUER: WHY I BLOG ON INSTAGRAM

Sarah Bauer (@lonelyroadlover) is a self-described digital nomad. She's a professional blogger in addition to blogging on Instagram. She has 1,500 Instagram followers and shares travel and personal life diary content and uses Instagram to highlight and direct her audience to posts to her blog. Her photography is outstanding, and her narratives range in length from a few sentences to a few paragraphs. She offers her experiences and insights into blogging on Instagram.

I started to use Instagram in 2016. My first steps were very much trial and error because I had to understand the medium first, and it took me some months to get a feeling for it. I did not really start blogging seriously until 2018, so when I started using Instagram in 2016, I just posted random travel photos with not much information and no links. I still received a lot of "likes," but more for my photography than for my content.

I got serious with my blog in February 2018. I tried to figure out how to use social media to direct more readers. I tried

Facebook, Instagram, and Pinterest and still maintain all three channels. On Facebook, I only reach Germans since hashtags aren't effective for attracting worldwide readers, and I have no time to feed several travel Facebook groups with my links. Pinterest turned out to be completely useless for me. My pins are seldom re-pinned, so they are almost never seen and therefore it hasn't helped generate more readers.

The most effective channel was and is Instagram.

What I did in the last 1–2 years: I try to post an inspirational mix of photos from my adventures and travels along with accomplishments, encouragement, and thoughts. When I'm on trips, I post 1–2 photos a day and otherwise share a photo every 1–3 days.

I also love to do little "24-Hour Stories," which more or less align with my photo-of-the-day. The photos are always accompanied by meaningful content because I want to let people know that these are more than "just nice photos" and that I have something to *say*. When I publish a new article on my blog, I use a special design for my Instagram posts that contain words on a photo (usually the headline of the blog article) and a frame and direct readers to the "link in bio." By now, people recognize the design means there is a new article on my blog, and it is not "just another photo."

The results: In the beginning, almost nobody clicked on the "link in bio" on my profile. It was quite discouraging. But after about a year I saw increasing numbers of people click on my profile and land on my blog when I posted the little word-frame-teaser with the referrer. I even have people who tell me they wait for them. In the past six months, I also repost the photo in my Instagram Story and again tell people that there is a new article on my blog. Unfortunately, there are no insights from Instagram that tell me if people end up on my blog after they have seen my story.

Another important thing is hashtags—what they are about and which target group they hit. I receive a lot of clicks, likes, and real readers on my blog when I post personal things about my unusual relationship and use hashtags like #LongDistanceRelationship or #AgeGapCouple. There seems to be a big readership when it comes to such topics. Other posts, for example, about Aruba where I used tags like #Aruba #TravelBlog or #Caribbean do not work so well. If it was only about generating more readers for my blog, I would need to stop writing about travel or home improvement and only write about love. But this is not my goal.

I do not make any money with my blog, and I do not want to (yet). I want to be free in my choice of topics and writing, and not become a slave of SEO and numbers. So, I will continue writing about topics that are not that popular and do not catch a lot of readers because they are *me*. And I want to be me on my blog.

The customer journey: Since I have nothing to sell and I do not promote my newsletter very much (only twenty subscribers), I do not really have that as a goal with my blog. My goal is truly just to move people, encourage and inspire them to live their lives to the fullest, work hard on their dreams, and be brave. Thankfully I receive more and more comments and notes telling me that people do feel inspired and encouraged. They *did* call their father after ten years of silence or finally renovated their old house because of one of my articles. This is such a reward, that it cannot be expressed by any numbers or money.

CHAPTER 8

CREATING YOUR PERSONAL BRAND

———

IN THIS CHAPTER:

Transparency Matters

Brand Perceptions

What's in a Name?

Changing Your Name

Anonymity

Aim for Consistency Across Channels

Begin with Your Bio

Getting Down to Business

Your Theme

Choosing Content Themes

Instagram Grid Layouts

BONUS: Examples of Themes and Grids

"The keys to brand success are self-definition,
transparency, authenticity and accountability."

— SIMON MAINWARING, AUTHOR

What if you didn't know the real names of your doctor, lawyer, or accountant? Unthinkable, right? Transparency and trust are two points to think about when you're in the process of setting up your profile and creating your personal brand on Instagram.

This book is about using Instagram as a blogging platform. However, it's worthwhile to think about elements used in creating your profile because it will help you plan your page's appearance and the positioning strategy when you launch your account. In this chapter, you'll learn about those and other aspects to think about that can impact how you're seen and perceived by your audience.

TRANSPARENCY MATTERS
Most of our social media acquaintances aren't on a parallel plane with professional or collegial relationships—but how about with your friends?

In 2008, when I began on Twitter, it wasn't unusual to see people using descriptive handles or "screen names" instead of their real names. I viewed it as a holdover from the days of bulletin and message boards when the internet was young, and screen names were *de rigueur*. This practice is still somewhat true on Instagram.

In the early 2000s, there were hugely popular personalities on social media using descriptive monikers or pseudonyms. As their accounts gained traction, many realized their growth potential was still ahead of them, and it didn't make sense to build recognition in an abstract screen name. So began the transition to using their real names and building equity in their personal brands.

I believe in transparency, which is why I use my real name across social platforms. I share content that reflects my point of view and what I value, and because my name is attached, it contributes to building trust.

BRAND PERCEPTIONS

Transparency matters when you're establishing yourself as a brand. Your name, your avatar (your profile picture), and consistency are as important as your behavior both on and offline. When you use your real name, you invite people to trust you. And by maintaining a consistent and positive presence across channels, you reinforce your authenticity as you develop relationships with people.

By building recognition of your name and avatar, you establish a "brand promise" that sets up what others can expect whenever they encounter you or your company online.

Relationships matter in personal life and in business. People *do* want to know who they are dealing with. By being transparent, the potential gain is greater than the risk.

WHAT'S IN A NAME?

Recognition is a form of currency, not only in social media but in business. Suppose a brand wants to enlist your collaboration as an influencer. In that case, they need assurance they're working with an authentic person with a stellar reputation. There are recognizable and respected people who use screen names but also self-identify using their real names. If you've been using a handle for a long time and have built equity in it, it makes sense to maintain it. But it's helpful and essential to include your real name *somewhere* in your profile. Here are several reasons why:

- You create a climate of trust by using your real name.
- You let people know who you are and how they can find you by name *or* by handle.
- You encourage more meaningful interactions when people know your name.
- By using your name, you build equity and recognition in your personal brand.

Clever and unique handles can be fun, but they can be problematic if they are not easily or *precisely* memorable. It can be especially true if you don't include your real name *anywhere*. For example, I had a Twitter connection who lives in the Baltimore area. I was going there on a business trip, and we agreed to meet for dinner. She is anonymous on social media and created an unusual name that meant something only to her, plus she didn't use her real name anywhere. We lost track of each other, and I wanted to reach out on Twitter, but I couldn't remember her moniker *or* name.

The substitution of numbers for letters may be great for building a password, but it's unrealistic to expect others to remember quirky spelling and configurations of your name. Special characters that require changing cases on a smart device (phones, tablets) are inconvenient for someone to type (including underscores, numbers, or other special characters). Although some applications will "autofill" a familiar name, it's better when you can avoid extra keystrokes.

CHANGING YOUR NAME

If you change it, your account will retain your friends and followers, but unless you've prepared them for the change, they may not recognize you.

If you need to change your handle, help your community by posting something about the name change in your profile, for example: "formerly @whatevermynamewas." You can also post an announcement of your intention and tag both names in the caption. People who are searching for you by name or former name will be able to find you. Success depends on whether enough people will remember your name in the first place. So, remember—use a name that is easy to remember.

ANONYMITY

A cloak of secrecy can signal more than a mystery. It could be related to someone's past or concerns about how their opinions could reflect on their jobs. Some people get their kicks hassling, menacing, or provoking people by "trolling" them. In a general sense, withholding one's real identity is a form of deception. With a proliferation of fake accounts on Instagram with names like "KeanuReeves12345," it doesn't instill a lot of confidence in the authenticity of an account.

Nefariousness isn't always the intention of a "nom de plume." I've noticed that millennials tend to use pseudonyms. When I've asked them why, the primary reason seems to be they don't want to be identified, judged, or held responsible for the content they post. I feel some of them don't want to be held accountable, or have their family or employers look up their accounts and see things they don't necessarily want to be seen.

But there are also legitimate reasons people conceal their identities. For example, maybe someone is in a custody battle and doesn't want to be found; maybe a person is hiding because they fear being stalked or menaced.

If serious issues are surrounding a person's safety, or if someone is evading creditors, what in the heck are they doing on social media except for the overwhelming feeling of "FOMO"—fear of missing out?

AIM FOR CONSISTENCY ACROSS CHANNELS

When you use the same name and avatar across social media, you reinforce your identity and recognition of your brand. Think of your avatar as your social media logo. If "Starbucks" used different names or logos on Facebook and Twitter, how would you recognize it?

You might know someone on Twitter by "@whatever," but if they send a friend request on Instagram using another name, you might not recognize them. In 2021, I created an account on a social media audio channel called Clubhouse. At the time, Clubhouse used Instagram as its "back channel" for messaging. (To backchannel is to communicate with others behind the scenes.) As of June 2021, Clubhouse doesn't have messaging built into the app, and since my Instagram profile picture doesn't match up with my usual identity, some people could wonder who I am. I've even missed a branding opportunity with Clubhouse users. When I started on Instagram, I created a personal account and used a unique avatar because I had no clue if it was a fad. I've now had it so long that I'm now afraid to change, so it has resulted in a branding misfire.

On most of my social media accounts, I use a version of my "Gravatar," a globally recognized image that represents me online (Gravatar, 2021). The color and design make me instantly recognizable in a feed. But I don't use the branded version on personal accounts where most are close friends, family, and real-life connections.

> *"If people like you they will listen to you, but if they trust you, they'll do business with you."*
>
> —ZIG ZIGLAR, AUTHOR

BEGIN WITH YOUR BIO

On any social media account, your bio tells people who you are and what you're about. It should reflect your personality and should offer people a way to connect. If you're blogging or journaling, you might want to "cross-pollinate" by enabling followers to follow other social media channels to help expand your reach. Or not! Maybe you want to fly under the radar for a while until you figure out what you're doing.

An Instagram bio has several pieces and needs to simultaneously accomplish several goals. The major components include:

- **Your Profile Photo**

Remember how I talked about transparency? Your profile picture is your chance to make a great first impression and let people know who they're following. Using an in-focus, well-lit image is appropriate. You might even consider having one professionally shot. Some Instagram users self-identify with their content. For example, a fan of dogs might choose a pug photo as their avatar. People quickly understand the shorthand, and if they like dogs and see a dog avatar, they'll check out your feed. Some users feel more comfortable using a symbolic image, but it engenders greater trust when a follower can see your face.

The size of the profile photo is precisely 110 x 110 pixels. Because web browsers and different devices have varying resolutions, it's better to use a slightly larger picture. In 2021, Hootsuite recommends profile pictures that are 320 x 320 pixels (Olafson and Tran, 2021).

- **Your Username**

A 30-character-long username is long! Keep in mind a long username takes space, and even though names will pop up in search after you type the first few characters, simple and shorter, easy to recall names are great.

- **Your Description**

A short description of up to 150 characters in length can quickly say who you are, what you do, and show your personality. Adding your location will help you make connections in your area and will help people who are looking to network with someone in your city. The description, along with your name and avatar and the images on your Instagram, make the case for why someone might be interested in following you. There's more about bio descriptions below.

- **Your Website Link**

Provide a way to be contacted, such as a website or email. The URL in your bio is the only clickable link. (I've mentioned a couple of multiple link resources, LinkTr.ee and Linkin.bio, that let you list multiple links.) If you include a URL, it's not counted in the 150 characters.

When it comes to strategies for writing a good bio, WordStream summarized some approaches and I've added a few more:

- Have a strong and concise value proposition.
- State the mission behind your business.
- Use humor when it fits your personality.
- Make it memorable.
- Show self-awareness.
- Be blunt, be bold, be inspiring.
- Make it short, sweet, and personable (Bond, 2021).

There is a useful article on Creative Bloq that discusses ways to create a perfect bio description. Among their recommendations:

- **Be succinct.** If a follower has no idea who you are, what are the essentials? Give a clue to what they might find in your feed. Depending on your goals, you could include your profession, interests, location, hashtags, or keywords.

- **Use Hashtags.** Limited numbers of hashtags are recommended, and I agree. But since hashtags are searchable, a few could help someone find their way to your page and content.

- **Emojis** add fun bits of information to your bio. They're eye-catching and reflect your personality. You can draw attention to your location by using the "pin" emoji (Android and iPhone emojis are different).

- **Line breaks.** You can break up your bio by featuring one kind of information per line. You can do this by immediately hitting "return" at the end of a line without inserting a space.

- **Include a CTA** (call to action). The CTA could link to your website or another social account or a link to your blog content (Hilder, 2019).

GETTING DOWN TO BUSINESS

Instagram business accounts have more features available to them than personal accounts. This is one of the reasons I converted my account from personal to business. Some of the features available and advantages of business accounts include:

- Adding a contact button leading to a phone number or email address.
- Adding a physical address.
- Instagram Story Highlights (Instagram Stories arranged in categories).
- Access to advertising tools.

- Access to insights about audience makeup, actions that are taken, and other data.
- For accounts with more than ten thousand followers—"swipable" links in Instagram Stories (a viewer can "swipe" or move the page up to reveal more information).
- Scheduling content in advance instead of loading it manually.
- Tagging products in posts and turning the feed into an online shop (West, 2021).

Business and e-commerce sites need to be on Instagram because customers search and follow their favorites. Fans and friends often tag photos with the brand name or brand hashtag. In digital marketing, this is called "UGC" or user-generated content, one of the most valuable ways of authentically amplifying your brand.

To convert a personal account to a business account, you'll need to convert your Instagram to a professional account. There are two types of business accounts:

- **Creator**—works best for public figures, artists, influencers, and content producers.

- **Business**—best for stores, brands, businesses, organizations, and service providers.

Your Instagram business page will need to connect to a corresponding Facebook business page. You'll need to choose a category that best describes what you do. (You'll have an option to show or hide the category on your profile.) A few samples:

- Artist
- Blogger
- Public Figure
- People
- Websites & Blogs

Business accounts can also become Instagram paying customers by running an ad or "boosting" a post. When you boost a post, you're paying to make a post more visible—even to people who aren't following you. Boosts raise awareness because more people will be exposed to your content.

Let's say you're an artist or author with a creator business profile on Instagram. Instagram can be a great discovery channel that can lead people to investigate and purchase. If you have a blog elsewhere, you can direct traffic there, too. The traffic on Google Analytics can be traced to the Instagram post when you add a UTM (Urchin Tracking Module) to your link. Note that links with a UTM are long and unwieldy, and it's recommended to use a service like Bit.ly (a free link-shortening service) to tidy up your links! (Simpson, 2020)

It took some effort when I switched to a business account, but it was worth it. The analytics alone offer insights you won't see with a personal account, and some of the scheduling options are exactly what you need when you're planning content that you want to deliver that aligns with dates, times, or events.

YOUR THEME

Just as it's true for an independent blog, on Instagram, it's beneficial to have a niche or theme. It helps visitors to your page understand what you share and decide their level of interest. What would be a good theme for you?

CHOOSING CONTENT THEMES

If you choose to go with a theme, it will help you curate your visual content. For example, if you want to be a gardening blogger, you can shoot or find photos and even build a backlog for future posts. Gardeners who blog on Instagram sometimes share pictures of what they're growing and describe it in their posts. Some offer tips or act as a resource for answering questions. The engagement helps grow their authority, as well as their plants.

Suppose you shoot images that reflect each post you write. If that's the case, you can unify the appearance of your grid through the use of filters or frames.

It's *your* Instagram feed, and you get to decide what you want to post.

SAMPLE CONTENT THEMES

There are too many to list, but here are some ideas:

- Fashion encompassing different styles and types
- Food including food bloggers, those who prepare food (recipes, instructions, etc.)
- Art, painting, professional photography; other media
- Cats, dogs, or animals in general
- Gardening, flowers, plants, nature
- Landscapes, seascapes, including sunrises, sunsets, and drone photography

- Quotes or quotes with images; typography
- Animated gifs featuring images or text
- Travel, architecture
- Macros of all types (typically nature, but I know someone who shoots macros of rusty objects!)
- Families and kids doing stuff
- Street photography
- Selfies (sounds tedious but yes, people shoot a million photos of themselves)
- Knitting (Yes, knitting!), crocheting, weaving, quilting, and other handcrafted arts

INSTAGRAM GRID LAYOUTS

The basic Instagram grid is row after row of three images separated by white "gutters," or spaces in between each shot. There are different ways to organize your grid, and some can be unique and unpredictable. An Instagram account that has a specific look, feel, and aesthetic is attractive. A common belief is that having a visual theme for your Instagram will help your account stand out. It's not as important at the beginning, and whatever you choose to do, you can change later. You just need to get started.

SAMPLE INSTAGRAM GRID LAYOUTS

- Use of the same filter on all of the images in your gallery
- Black and white photography or duotone/quadtone photos
- Pastel color palette
- Bright color palette
- High-definition photos—where images are extra detailed and saturated

- Flat lays—a styled shot taken from overhead, looking down
- Tiling—dividing a single image into six to nine sections on your grid, or using three images to create a horizontal line
- Puzzle—breaking up a single-image collage into tiles
- Checkerboard—alternates between images and quotes or colors
- Borders—consistently using the same frames for the photos in your gallery

To give you an idea of how content themes and grid layouts might look, I've included some samples below. Users find creative ways of sharing content that attract attention and draw people into their posts.

BONUS: EXAMPLES OF THEMES

One of the most effective ways to unify the look of your grid (the rows of images on your profile that appear 3-across) is by focusing on a specific category of content. But choosing a filter and using it consistently across your content is equally effective. Instagram has built-in options for different types of frames and filters. When you're new on the platform, there is a temptation to try all of them. You should experiment to see what you like. When I was just starting out, I thought almost all the built-in filters were awesome!

Following are samples of themes including food (Sean and Penelope @globalrecharge), landscapes (Ryan Hodges @ryanintheus), fashion (Diana Horsfall @queenhorsfall), and quotes (Rachel Thompson @rachelintheoc).

@queenhorsfall is a fashion blogger and brand influencer with 54K followers. She shoots and art directs her content. She began experimenting with some of her own filter combinations and created a distinctively different look. She is featured in the photos and the changes in look and feel to add texture to her grid. This part of her Instagram shows horizontal stripes with three photos across that are related to a location, color, or filter.

She writes:

"After moving from Europe to Korea, it awakened a sleeping passion that was influenced by Korean fashion. I met a fashion blogger who inspired me to create an account where I could share my personal style.

We moved to the US, and what began as a hobby grew into a business. I started to receive invitations from brands that were willing to pay me to feature their fashions.

Ever-evolving changes to the algorithms, and fashion accounts that invested money to grow their followings, made it difficult to compete. I went back to using Instagram as a platform to connect with people who truly wanted to know me as a person. I still enjoy the app for feeling closer to the world."

—DIANA HORSFALL @QUEENHORSFALL

EXAMPLES OF GRIDS

An identifiable look and feel can be accomplished through the style of your grid and a consistent use of filters or frames. One of the most creative grids on Instagram is one created by Jack Higgins. @jackandpele has 1,400 followers. His Instagram encompasses the thoughts and people in Jack's orbit. In the following samples from his feed, he uses a variety of visually creative techniques. Each section of his Instagram tells a story and is fully enjoyed the most when viewed on his grid. Those who follow him understand the appearance of white boxes in their feed signal; there is something happening on his grid.

"Since 1997, when the term was first used, blogging has come to represent every imaginable online category of online thought, whether written or pictured, that is updated. People on Twitter, Instagram, or Facebook say they are blogging. I have my great, great grandmother's diary. If she was still alive making entries, she would tell you she is blogging."

— JACK HIGGINS @JACKANDPELE ADVERTISING
AND MARKETING, MARCH 30, 2021

Following are grid samples including a random puzzle and a modified checkerboard combination (Jack Higgins), black and white (Cheryl Senter @cherylsenter), and panoramas with white borders (Yohann @y.l.l.y).

Anyone who starts an Instagram account will discover what they love the most. No one shares the same type of content in the same way forever. For many years, I shared random content and played around with apps that changed the look or feeling of my images. Eventually, I discovered I had two favorite things: nature and cats. A friend once told me my "thing" is flowers, and I was in denial about it because I felt I was much more than that! I realized she was somewhat correct because when my images veered too far from nature (or cats) I could tell my posts weren't being shown to as many people. I began shooting more macros, but also noticed that when I "stayed in my lane" Instagram rewarded me. It took a few years before I settled into a look and feel of my posts. I have mostly maintained a straightforward grid. I now primarily use one app and have a "recipe" that I apply to establish visual consistency. I share my personal formula in the next chapter.

CHAPTER 9

IF YOU BUILD IT, THEY WILL COME

IN THIS CHAPTER:

Image Types

Basic Smartphone Photo Tips

Apps for Android and iOS

Beyond Image Editing

Writing Your Post

Hashtags

Optional Actions to Enhance Visibility and Engagement

Algorithms

BONUS: How I Shoot the Photos in My Gallery

"Nobody will see what you're writing unless you allow it, but even you can't see what you're writing unless you start."

"If you build it, he will come" is a quote from the 1989 film *Field of Dreams*. The movie is about wanting and believing in something and doing everything possible to make it come true. Think of your Instagram blog as *your* field of dreams.

Maybe you've given some thought to how you'd like to blog on Instagram. Whether it will be a journal, a way to drive traffic to your blog, or maybe the ultimate destination for your posts. Whatever you decide, the main parts of your post will include the image and the text (including hashtags). Let's look at the pieces of a post.

IMAGE TYPES

In 2019, research showed:

- 68 percent of users were posting a single image.
- 18 percent posted videos.
- 14 percent posted "carousels," multiple images revealed when the viewer "swipes" or moves an image to the left (Michalski, 2019). In 2021, Carousels are now number 1.

According to personal preference, some use filters or stack multiple filters to create effects. Some users are purists and leave photos in their original state. (The hashtags,

#NoFilter or #NoFilterNeeded are often added to unaltered images.)

I'm an amateur photographer who takes pictures with my smartphone and doesn't know how to use a full-featured camera. Because of Instagram, I see the ability to shoot and share photography as a skill within reach of anyone. You can look like a professional photographer even if you only use Instagram's built-in filters.

Choosing an image "niche" can help attract an audience. Photography website Pixobo lists thirteen popular photo categories that result in more likes and follows on Instagram.

- Landscape images, panoramic, and wildlife photos
- Aerial, architecture, and urban
- Event and sports
- Portraits and beauty
- Macro
- Abstract
- Black and white, infrared, or Lomo
- Past and present
- Candid
- Conceptual
- Still life
- Tilt-shift
- Vintage (Bates, 2019)

There are surprising numbers of nonvisual users on Instagram. If you are among them, don't despair because you will have plenty of company. You'll read how nonphotographers can carve out a visual presence on the platform.

BASIC SMARTPHONE PHOTO TIPS

Your photos will look best if they are in focus and shot in natural light. Photos usually look more pleasing when you *don't use the flash*. It's 2020, and more smartphone cameras have made improvements to compensate for low light. Google Pixel, iPhone, Samsung, and others have made it possible to shoot in low light with outstanding results.

HOW TO SHOOT IN LOW LIGHT

If you have an older smartphone, low light can create challenges for focusing. In a low-light situation, using a tripod will help stabilize your camera and result in a better image.

HOW TO FOCUS

On most phone cameras, tap the area of the screen you want to be sharp. The camera focus circle or box will appear, and the lens will adjust and preview the shot. If you anchor your phone against a solid, upright surface, like a table or wall or door jamb, then tap the focus, your photos will be in focus *and* perpendicular to your horizon line. If you're shooting "hand-held" (not mounted or anchored), the key is to be as still as you can. To improve the sharpness of a hand-held shot, hold your upper arms against your body and hold your breath to reduce movement when you shoot.

HOW TO BE A STRAIGHT SHOOTER

I can't say this enough: Be aware of shooting straight. Skewed photos are more evident where there is a horizon line (like a lake against a mountain backdrop). The same applies to buildings that lean. Instagram and other photo editing apps have an option to "rotate" an image to correct it, so it's not a big deal. But it's best to get it right in the camera because you may end up clipping part of your image when you try to level or straighten it later. Alternatively, you may purposely tilt your camera to achieve an artistic effect, which is perfectly okay!

EDITING PHOTOGRAPHS

It's possible to correct lighting in Instagram. You can take under or over-exposed photos and often still make them work.

Instagram's brightness adjustment can improve dark photos. Still, it's helpful if you have some highlight and shadow detail in the first place. If you shoot with available daylight (but not in direct sunlight), it's likely your images will be fine. You might find your images become grainy at night or in low light and be tempted to shoot with a flash but doing so usually results in harsh lighting. Is there a solution? Instead, and if possible, move your subject closer to a light source.

An average person can produce beautiful photos using Instagram's built-in filters and additional tools. It's a magical experience to see your photos come to life through adjustments and filters. Sixty percent of top brands use the same filter for every post. It enables your content to have a consistent look and feel throughout your timeline (Gotter, 2021).

In addition to Instagram's built-in filters, there are apps and filters available to explore. I've downloaded dozens, but at the end of the day, I only use a few. Some apps are available only on iPhones, and others are only on Androids, but many work for both. Editing applications can rescue a lot of photos.

APPS FOR ANDROID AND IOS

If you're looking for a solution or want to achieve a specific effect, enter search terms on the Play Store or App Store by searching "photo editor." You can find an app for almost any image editing need. There are more apps listed in the Resources section at the back of this book.

Here are a few apps I've used for making corrections, adjustments, cropping, and filtering images:

- **Snapseed** (Android & iOS)—my favorite. This free app has an easy-to-use interface and a great selection of twenty-nine tools and filters that enable beautiful photos.

- **Pixlr** (online, Android & iOS) offers more control in image editing and boasts more than two million combinations of free filters, overlays and effects.

- **VSCO** (Android & iOS) is a free photo editing tool with ten free presets. Video, Montage, and access to 200+ presets requires membership.

- **Adobe Lightroom** (Android & iOS) free with in-app purchases, offers powerful and simple-to-use features for beginners or advanced users.

Depending on the app, you'll find options to:

- Edit raw files
- Straighten horizon lines
- Alter colors
- Remove blemishes
- Adjust highlight and shadow details
- Sharpen or blur
- Use filters to enhance or add interest
- Intensify colors
- Adjust curves
- Alter the depth of field
- Convert color to black and white
- Correct perspective

BEYOND IMAGE EDITING

Some apps will make people look younger, older, slimmer, or change genders (search for Face Swap Apps). Additionally, there are apps to create memes, collages, and create special effects. Here are a few useful apps I've tried:

- **Boomerang** (Android & iOS)—easily create mini looping videos.

- **Touch of Color** (iOS)—selectively changes colors in your images.

- **Canva** (Online, Android & iOS)—more than image editing, Canva can make anyone feel like they're a graphic designer.

- **Prisma** (Android & iOS)—converts a photo into a work of art.

You can find volumes of advice about how to shoot and edit photos for sharing on social media. With a little creativity, some of the worst-quality images can still capture a moment in time. Just take pleasure in the surprises you discover once you're processing your photos, then share them for others to enjoy! You'll find more image and content resources in Chapter 12.

WRITING YOUR POST

Earlier, we looked at several styles of blogging. Someone new to Instagram is in the perfect place to try different approaches to storytelling or change the look and feel of their Instagram feed. In the beginning, when you have fewer followers, it's a great time to experiment.

YOUR TOPIC AND CTA

In writing your first blog post, start with this basic approach:

- Decide on the topic of your post and what you want to say.
- Consider how to draw in readers by asking them to share their experiences, or
- Ask your readers to answer a question.

One way you can make a post relatable is to end it with a question or request. In a broad sense, your question or request is the equivalent of a CTA (call to action) in a blog post. It's the part of your post that invites engagement.

MECHANICS OF WRITING

Following your username, you have about ninety characters to write the "teaser" at the very beginning of your post. That's the number of letters and spaces that will preview on most devices before the rest of the copy breaks for "...more." Creating an exciting or intriguing lead-in could make the difference between someone continuing to read your post versus only viewing the image.

Your post has a maximum character length of 2,200 characters (or about three hundred words), including your username, spaces, emojis, hidden characters, and invisible characters like a hard return or "line break." In addition to the character limit, a post can include up to thirty hashtags.

Applications such as Microsoft Word are helpful because you can hammer out a draft, and it's easy to check on the character count and run spell-check. When I can, I'll try to compose this way because invariably, I miss something when I write directly on the phone. If you happen to notice a typo in your post after the fact, never fear. You can go back and make corrections. (Instagram notes when a post has been edited.)

Line breaks help separate ideas in your post and make it more readable. Some bloggers on Instagram compose their posts in one solid block. It's easier for them to write their posts that way, but it makes their posts more difficult to read. There are methods of creating a line break by inserting a "return" at the end of a line, but I've found it doesn't always work. Some will use a period or emoji on their own line between paragraphs.

I've found two apps that do an excellent job of creating nice, clean breaks:

- **Instagram Text Spacer** is available to use on the web.

- **Instaspacer** is available on Android and iOS.

You can type or paste your copy into one of the apps, then copy and paste it into Instagram with beautiful line breaks. The process is simple, and the result is clean.

HASHTAGS

What is a hashtag? Hashtags originated on Twitter as a shortcut to help locate tweets about specific topics. Tweets are quoted in the news every day, so I think they are generally understood. But just in case you don't know, on Instagram and elsewhere, a hashtag is a word or phrase preceded by the hash (#) symbol that signals the contents of your post.

The importance of hashtags can't be understated. In one of my posts, 860 views occurred because of hashtags. When users are searching for a particular topic, hashtags will lead them to the most recent or top posts associated with the hashtag.

Users with fewer than twenty-five thousand followers benefit the most from hashtags. In 2019, posts with 10+ hashtags reaped an additional 6 percent engagement rate, which is a great indicator they work (Later and Fohr, 2020).

One way to find popular hashtags is to type in a descriptor, and you'll see a list of the most popularly used hashtags related to your search term. For example, if you type in #Cat, a list will pop up with #Cat and related hashtags, each showing the number of times it has been used.

Choose hashtags that reflect your content. According to Later, "Instead of using the most popular hashtags, it's better to use the top hashtags that have an engaging community behind them and are specific to your audience" (Warren 2020). General hashtags like #Cat have a lot of competition. Hashtags can be very "niche," and if you think of a way to describe your content and search for it, you might be surprised to find others are using the same hashtag.

SocialPilot says it's best to use a combination of short and "long-tail" hashtags. Short hashtags (like #Cat) have the highest search volume, but long-tail hashtags like "#MaineCoonKittensforSale" are more targeted to a specific audience.

Whatever you do, it's good to mix things up. Instagram's algorithm penalizes those who use the same hashtags for every post. Using appropriate, relevant hashtags will be more effective and keep you from being shadowbanned (Newberry, 2021).

If you create a branded hashtag for yourself, it will enable you to keep tabs on your posts and make it easier to search for your content or see if others have used it. The hashtag could be #YourName or #YourAccountName (fill in with your name, of course).

Is there an easy way to find a list of hashtags? There are aggregators on the web, but they can come with a risk:

banned hashtags may be lurking in the lists you find. When you use a banned hashtag, Instagram suppresses the visibility of your post or may remove it. If the hashtag is *verboten*, Instagram could ban your account. Instagram bans hashtags for several reasons:

- If they represent content depicting self-harm
- Sexual content
- Illegal behaviors

And, if content using specific hashtags has been reported as inappropriate, it can result in a user being either temporarily or permanently banned (Lee, 2021).

To find if a hashtag is banned in the Instagram app, just tap the magnifying glass icon, which will open a search bar. You'll see several tabs (top, account, tags, location). By selecting the "tags" tab, you can type in the #Hashtag you want to check out. Tap on the hashtag, and if it's banned, you'll see a message to that effect.

OPTIONAL ACTIONS TO ENHANCE VISIBILITY AND ENGAGEMENT

TAG PEOPLE
Tagging people (using their "@names") helps ensure they'll see your post. If you tag someone in a regular post, they'll probably see it at some point, but if you tag someone in an Instagram Story, they'll see it only if they check their notifications. There is currently a limit of tagging a maximum of twenty people per post.

SHARE TO OTHER CHANNELS

Before you hit "share," you have the option to post your content to other platforms, including Facebook, Twitter, and Tumblr. If you have a business account, the share will go to your business Facebook page, but if it's personal, it will appear on your Facebook feed. Instagram no longer supports sharing posts to Twitter, so your post will appear as a text preview. You can share to Tumblr, another blogging and social networking platform, with great results, but it will show only the first image of a carousel.

It's possible to share your Instagram post over a text message, email or other channels by clicking the three dots located at the top right of the post. It will give you options to share in several ways and allow you to copy the direct link to the post so you can share elsewhere.

GEOTAG YOUR LOCATION

One of the final steps is to tag your location. Geotagging is an electronic tag that identifies the place where a photo has been taken. Posts with a location tag receive 79 percent more engagement (Barnhart, 2021).

Your post could surface when the location is searched. Or a person who notices the location tag could click on it, which gives users the option to see the location on a map. For example, after viewing a photo tagged with "Jardins du Chateau de Versailles," I tapped the location name. It took me to a map showing where it is located and listed the top and most recent photos taken there. In addition, I could tap a button that says, "More Information," which in this case identified the location category, its website, and a telephone number. Very handy! Also, the location creates an opportunity to discover and follow users in your area. The location information appears right above the image and is quickly conveyed to your audience.

HOW TO POST ON INSTAGRAM

1. Tap the + icon

2. Navigate to your photo library and choose a photo, or shoot one using the Instagram app

3. Move the photo by pressing your fingers on it until the crop is in the position you like

4. Hit "Next"

5. Choose a filter

6. Type a caption

7. Add hashtags to optimize your post

8. Tag friends

9. Add your location

10. Share to Instagram and share to other platforms (Facebook, Twitter, Tumblr

ALGORITHMS

Mathematically speaking, an algorithm is a problem-solving process often followed by computers. In social media, algorithms sort the posts that a user sees according to what it *thinks* a user will like instead of when it is published. In 2020, Later indicated six factors that influenced the Instagram algorithm (the way the platform sorts posts and delivers them to you).

The main factor is the prediction that it is showing you photos you will want to see. The algorithm changes because the feed ranking adapts, improves, and learns based on the data it collects via machine learning (Warren, 2021). But some key influencing elements include:

- **Interest**—based on what you've liked in the past

- **Relationship**—posts by friends, family, and those you care about

- **Timeliness**—considers how long ago a post was shared

- **Frequency**—how often do you open the app?

- **Following**—you can't see everything if you follow a lot of people

- **Usage**—the more you use the app, the more you'll see

Historically, the Instagram feed would show users images in chronological order, so current posts would appear at the top and older posts would be somewhat buried. Changes in the algorithm mean the content you see often is the result of the relationships you have with your community.

The Instagram algorithm is like a living, breathing thing that grows and changes. As I mentioned earlier in the book, in April of 2019, "likes" were hidden in selected markets. The initiative was in response to an episode of "Black Mirror," a dystopian British TV series, where all human interactions were rated on a scale of 1 to 5 stars. After two years of testing, in May 2021, Instagram once again made likes visible, but now each person can choose to hide them (Newton, 2021).

FREQUENCY

It used to be a best practice to post daily as an individual and more often as a brand. Instagram's algorithm has favored people who post regularly and those who engage through likes, comments, and shares. According to Later and Fohr, the number one finding in their 2020 study on influencer marketing was that quality outperforms quantity on the Instagram grid. Upon analyzing data, it found posting schedules were shifting, and users were posting less frequently. The reduction in frequency was attributed to the time and energy required to create an impactful post.

Influencers with 250,000-500,000 followers were identified as exceptions to this trend. The advantage of posting more frequently is that posts likely appear more often in their followers' feeds.

Whether you post daily or choose to share less frequently, the two-pronged approach of using images to catch attention and writing a lead to draw in your audience, will help make the most of the times when you decide to share.

POST ENGAGEMENT

When you're building your community, a more effective action is to hit "reply" and post a response, like how you might if you were conversing with that person. As noted earlier in the book, using someone's name in a reply requires a bit of extra effort, but it's more personal and meaningful.

Logistically there may be times when you don't have time to respond to every comment. Some users completely turn off comments. Users who routinely turn off comments have their own reasons for doing so, but it boils down to putting a low priority on engagement.

SEO and digital marketing specialist tool, Mondovo, says comments build "social proof" that you have an engaged audience. Reciprocal interaction is personally satisfying, but it's also attractive to advertisers searching for influencers. Quickly responding to comments improves your chances of ranking as a top post when a hashtag is searched. Top posts increase the opportunity to attract more people to your page and build social proof to attract more followers (Elsley, 2019).

BONUS: HOW I SHOOT THE PHOTOS IN MY GALLERY

In the personal brand chapter, I talk about ways to create a style for your gallery. When someone visits your profile page, they'll see nine to twelve of your most recent posts organized in a grid. By applying a similar visual treatment to your content, visitors can get a sense of your aesthetics. You'll recognize when you hit on the right combination of filters or actions, so have some fun and explore some of the possibilities.

My images have a distinct look and are recognizable in the feed. I shoot many macros and nature photos in portrait mode (recommended to me by @queenhorsfall), which is a great way to achieve an interesting effect. Portrait mode captures a shallow depth of field, where part of the shot (your subject) is in focus, and the rest of the image appears soft and blurry, also known as bokeh.

I'm going to explain step-by-step what I do to create the style used in my gallery. The app I use most often is Snapseed. The steps might look complicated, but it only takes me ten or fifteen minutes to adjust most photos.

OPEN A PHOTO IN SNAPSEED

If I notice an imperfection, like dirt on a flower petal, I'll first open "TOOLS" and select "Healing." It's possible to remove blemishes or, depending on the photo, objects that obstruct the shot can be removed. Once I've fixed the problem, I tap the checkmark. ✓

Next in TOOLS, depending on what I want to correct, I might choose:

- Tune Image
- Details
- Curves
- White Balance
- Rotate

In TOOLS, there's also a brush tool to "dodge and burn," and filters plus other adjustment options. When I'm happy with the adjustments, I tap the checkmark. ✓

- Next, in TOOLS, I select:
- "HDR Scape," and "Nature"
- I adjust the filter strength to about 13 percent, then tap the checkmark. ✓

In TOOLS, next I select "Glamour Glow," and depending on the photo, adjust the slider from 25 percent to 100 percent, then tap the checkmark ✓ when I'm happy. It's possible to adjust the degree of glow, saturation and warmth, but sometimes after applying this step, I find the shot is too saturated for my taste. To fine-tune further, I go back to TOOLS, and again select "Tune Image," where I can adjust:

- Brightness
- Contrast
- Saturation
- Ambience
- Highlights

- Shadows, or
- Warmth

The final step is to go to "Export" and select "Save." There are other export options depending on your workflow preference.

Another menu option called "LOOKS" offers an array of preset filter combinations. The first choice is "Last Edits," which will automatically apply the same adjustments (beyond retouching) to your next photo. You can explore various looks, and if you find a preset you like, you can choose to use it across your gallery to create a unified style.

It sometimes feels like there are too many apps and options. If you're overwhelmed, start simply by posting an image and don't worry about image-enhancement steps. Once you feel comfortable sharing a photo or other content, you'll feel empowered to try things to make your content even better!

CHAPTER 10

LIGHTS, CAMERA, ACTION!

————

IN THIS CHAPTER:

Visual Options

Video (various formats)

Identify What and How You Want to Share

BONUS: A Reels Conversation

"In a world where we have too many choices and too little time, the obvious thing to do is just ignore stuff."

—SETH GODIN, AUTHOR, ENTREPRENEUR

I t's not nice to ignore people, but how about when you ignore *things*? When it comes to Instagram, the algorithm rewards those who use Instagram's shiny, new features through more prominent visibility of their posts. And those who ignore the new features? Well, Instagram doesn't think it's as nice.

Seth Godin's quote is apropos because Instagram started as a photo-sharing app but has evolved to offer more content creation choices. It developed new features to compete with new, fun social media apps, especially those focused on short-form videos, such as TikTok and Snapchat. Users can now create similar content directly on Instagram without ever leaving the platform.

However, having too many choices can be stressful! This chapter contains *more* image-sharing options currently available on Instagram. I realize this could feel a little overwhelming when this book is about *blogging* on Instagram. Still, to be fair, some of you might find video to be your sweet spot, so these options are good to understand.

VISUAL OPTIONS

The most basic option is to post a photo, video, or series of pictures and videos in your feed. This chapter contains an overview of video formats, but I'm also going to spend time on Boomerang and Carousels, two features that are built into the Instagram app.

BOOMERANG

Boomerang is an app that lets you create animated GIFs (Graphics Interchange Format). By taking a series of ten image frames that are stitched together and played in sequence, Boomerang forms a short moving picture. If you've seen short videos that loop or repeat back and forth, they might be products of Boomerang. Boomerang videos can be fun on your feed, in an Instagram Story, or saved and used elsewhere.

HOW TO CREATE A BOOMERANG
FOR INSTAGRAM STORIES

1. Open Instagram.

2. Tap the "+" symbol.

3. Choose "Story."

4. Select the "infinity" symbol.

5. Record new content by holding down the camera button to shoot a burst of pictures.

6. Add effects, apply filters, add text, or draw. You can adjust the sound (on or off) and have a chance to view or edit it before publishing it to your Story.

7. Click "Next" and choose to share your Story or send it directly to friends (Stanton, 2021).

You can also turn your "Live photos" into Boomerangs! Boomerang is also a standalone app available on the App Store or Google Play.

CAROUSEL

A carousel is a post that shares up to ten photos or videos at once. Carousels not only invite engagement, but they extend your page's reach. Carousel posts drew up to 5.13 percent higher engagement than one-image or one-video posts (Pearce, 2021).

> *"[In 2021] the type of post with the*
> *highest median number of likes and*
> *comments goes to carousel posts."*
>
> —(HUBSPOT, MENTION, 2021)

I love carousel posts for many reasons, but the first is the excellent engagement rate and volume of positive feedback I receive. I curate a slide show of three to six images to share with my weekly post. The first image in the sequence should be your best shot because it's the part of your post that grabs attention and draws a viewer into the lead of your caption.

Instagram's algorithm rewards engagement, so the longer a viewer spends on your content, the more likely your post will show up in the feed. If you add relevant hashtags, your post could even make it to the "Explore" page, where recommended content pops up when a user searches.

In a carousel, viewers swipe through a series of pictures that take more time than to view a single photo, so it naturally increases engagement. I found a hidden benefit: If followers view only the first image without "swiping left," to see the others, your content re-appears in their feed, next time showing the second image. Because the subsequent images from the carousel pop up again in my followers' feeds, my carousel posts often result in additional comments, sometimes made by someone who has already commented.

Another reason to consider a carousel is that it can help prevent someone from muting you. Muting is used to suppress accounts you don't want to "unfollow," but shares content you're not interested in. It's also good for hiding those who tend to share too much too quickly. When a user posts several individual photos in a short time, their "noise" interferes with seeing other people's content. If you decide to mute someone, you can choose to mute posts, Instagram Stories, or both. I usually choose to mute posts to continue seeing their (less frequent) content in Instagram Stories.

Although carousels can have a combination of photos and videos, everything will have the same shape. There are work-arounds to have your carousel content vary from square to landscape to portrait, but it requires learning how to manipulate the shape of the preview for the content.

Here's an interesting factoid: Video clips can be up to sixty seconds long, so ten sequential clips essentially result in a ten-minute video.

It's super easy to post multiple Instagram photos at once. Here's an overview:

HOW TO CREATE A CAROUSEL OF MULTIPLE IMAGES

Choose from two to ten photos that you would like to share in the same post. If you want to take the images and first edit in an app like Pixlr, go ahead and do that, or you can edit directly in Instagram using its built-in filters, frames and effects.

Once you know which images you want to share, hit the **double-square icon** in the lower right corner, which tells Instagram that you intend to select additional photos.

When choosing the first photo, the number "1" will indicate it's the first one you chose, when choosing the next, it will have a number "2" and so on.

NOTE: In mid-2021, some users are unable to access the double-square icon and need to press and hold their finger on a single image before being shown an option to select multiple photos (Bernardini, 2021).

Arrange the Order of Your Images

You can change the sequence of the images by pressing the **white circle with diagonal hash marks** in the lower-left corner. It will allow you to move a photo from one position to another. At this time, you can apply various Instagram filters to the images if you haven't already preprocessed them elsewhere. If you don't want to use a filter, no worries! Just move on to the next image by hitting "Next." You can tweak the filters if you change your mind, and you can apply different filters to each photo.

Final Steps of Posting a Carousel

Next, you can tag other users, choose the geographic location, and if you've linked your account to Facebook, Twitter or Tumblr, you have an option to share your content to the channels you choose. Insert your blog post and hashtags, then it's time to post! The final post shows your username, the location, and the first photo will have "dots" ••• underneath it. The dots indicate the number of pictures in the post.

VIDEO (VARIOUS FORMATS)

There are several ways to post video content, including:

- Instagram Stories
- IGTV
- Reels
- Instagram Live

Videos typically receive up to twice as much engagement as a photo. They are one of the best ways to increase visibility and engagement. It has become easy and accessible for accounts with small budgets to tap into the power of video through Instagram Stories, IGTV, Instagram Live, and Reels. Videos allow users to share more in-depth stories that a single photo or even a carousel can't easily communicate. For a blogger on Instagram, videos can give audiences a chance to get to know you.

The aspect ratio (the relationship between the width and height) for videos is a minimum of:

- 1.91:1 (1080 pixels wide x 608 pixels high) to 4:5 (1080 x 1350)

What does that mean? The 1.91:1 shape is a wide rectangle, such as you would get if you shot your video with your camera oriented horizontally. The 4:5 ratio is a vertical rectangle, such as you would get when holding your camera vertically.

Instagram supports videos that have a width between 320px and 1080px. So, if your video is smaller than 320px, Instagram will enlarge it to fit, and if it exceeds 1080px, Instagram will resize it to fit.

INSTAGRAM TV

IGTV is Instagram's version of YouTube and is a way for you to be discovered through creating and sharing original video content that shows you doing what you love to do. Longer videos allow you to explain, educate, or showcase a product. The content works to build your community and engagement. It's even possible to create a series and playlists focused on topics or themes (Glover, 2020).

Before creating videos for IGTV, you need to create a channel, which you can do by using the IGTV app. You can upload a video from your camera roll, add a title, description, and links. The links take users outside of the app! Verified accounts can share video content up to sixty minutes in length, but for most users, the maximum is fifteen minutes (Warren, 2021).

IGTV gives users a place to post videos from one to 15 minutes in length and share them on Instagram. The format began as only vertical, but now it is both

- Vertical 9:16 (1080 x 1920) like your smartphone, or

- Horizontal with an aspect ratio of 16:9 (1920 x 1080) like most widescreen TVs and computer monitors

You should check the size and shape when you share a preview of your IGTV with your followers. In the feed, it will show up cropped to 4x5. The preview crops to 1:1 (square) in your profile grid, so it's good to keep the "live matter" like headline type and important visual content in the center of the preview.

Automatic closed captions make IGTV videos accessible to deaf and hard of hearing viewers and make the content available to more people. It will provide more relevance to viewers who consume videos with the sound turned off (Rev, 2021).

INSTAGRAM STORIES
Instagram Stories was modeled after Snapchat's ephemeral 24-hour-lifespan content. Stories create awareness of your brand and content, and they lead to more engagement. You

can incorporate videos, photos, and text plus various filters, animations, emojis, stickers, interactive elements, and music. I try to post Instagram Stories when I can because of its short lifespan (it disappears in 24 hours) creates urgency, and your followers may be inclined to check them out.

For your content to occupy the whole screen without borders, the recommended aspect ratio is: 9:16 (1080 x 1920) or the full vertical screen of your smartphone.

New stories appear in a stories bar at the top of your feed and will sometimes also appear in a highlighted bar as you scroll through your content. Stories are easy to create, share, and maintain your presence. If you aren't posting regularly on your grid, you can share a story and remind your followers of your account. I frequently find myself checking out stories, then clicking on a use's profile which takes me to their profile page. It's an easy way to catch up with some of my favorite people and catch up on posts I've missed.

After using Instagram for a while, most users realize a "story" is short-term content, so they're inclined to check it out right away. Stories let viewers react quickly through emojis, yes or no, and other fun mechanisms, so it's a low-demand way to experience some quick engagement. A disadvantage of posting a story is, if you are tagged in a story but didn't see the notification in a timely fashion, it's no longer available once twenty-four hours has passed.

It always struck me as a waste of energy to create content that disappears in twenty-four hours! But in the case of Instagram, there are ways to store copies in your photo library.

If you have a business account, you can also archive stories in categories you've chosen to appear on your home screen.

Those with more than ten thousand followers have access to a feature that lets them include a link for a call to action (CTA). My account has fewer than ten thousand followers, so I can't post an actionable link using the "swipe up" feature in Instagram Stories. HubSpot shared an ingenious solution: Use IGTV as a workaround! Check out the sidebar that follows!

HOW TO ADD A LINK TO YOUR INSTAGRAM STORY WHEN YOU HAVE FEWER THAN 10K FOLLOWERS

The majority (53 percent) of users on Instagram are not verified and have fewer than one thousand followers, so for most of us, it's not possible to add a live link to an Instagram Story. However, it's possible to get around the ten thousand follower minimum requirement by using IGTV.

To add a link to your Instagram Stories:

- Create an IGTV video drawing attention to your video's title (e.g., "Tap on the title to get the link!")
- Add the link to your IGTV caption.
- Post the video to your IGTV channel.
- Open Instagram Stories.

- Click the link icon at the top of the screen.

- Select +IGTV Video.

- Select the IGTV video you just created (MacLachlan, 2021).

This workaround will let viewers click the link in your IGTV caption!

INSTAGRAM LIVE

Have you heard of "live streaming?" For immediate engagement, try live streaming to your audience using an "Instagram Live" video.

Instagram live videos are vertical and will always occupy your screen's full width and height without any borders. The aspect ratio is typically 9:16.

Your followers can choose to receive a notification that will appear at the top of their screen when you start an Instagram Live. In the same top bar that shows recent Instagram Stories, Instagram superimposes a small red box on your icon with the word "LIVE," so your audience realizes you're live streaming. Sometimes you can see an Instagram Live topic above your feed. You can decide if it's relevant to you, and if you're curious, this is your cue to click on it, pop in and watch, ask to join, or leave if it's not exciting or relevant.

Audiences can like, make comments, send emojis, and interact with your live feed. If you decide to try Instagram Live, it can be helpful to have another person with you who can keep track of questions people ask so you can respond. There are control settings to help ensure a positive experience (filtering offensive comments, for example). When it's over, it shares automatically to your Instagram Story for twenty-four hours. Still, if you want to archive it, you can share on IGTV, or download your video. You can also delete it! (West, 2021)

REELS

Reels is Instagram's version of "TikTok." Reels gives you an excellent opportunity to get comments and start conversations. The video clips are fifteen to thirty seconds and can be set to music using Instagram's database. Within Instagram, you can find music that is free to use in your content.

Reels are vertical videos viewed in the same aspect ratio as Live and IGTV: 9:16 (1080 x 1920).

You'll find Reels in the "+" New Post menu which lists "Post," "Story," "Reels," and "Live." When you choose Reels, you'll see a menu of options to add music, set a time of fifteen or thirty seconds, adjust the speed, add effects, touch up the image, and set a timer. You can also record your own, original audio.

Just decide on the length of your video, then record! You can set a countdown timer, so you know when to start, and if you'd like to start and stop several times, you can do that by pressing and holding the record button. Once you're happy with the result, you can draw, add stickers, choose a thumbnail cover, share to stories, and explore the feed and the reels tabs on your profile. Your published reels are found on the reels tab of your profile.

Of the video options, Reels will have the most significant impact on the visibility of your account, and you could find it's one of the easiest ways to share video. All the options are ways to remind your audience that you exist. If using video increases the chance of someone visiting or following your Instagram profile—all the better!

The video options can all work to establish and promote your brand, generate interest, and connect transparently with your audience. But don't feel pressured to start shooting videos in addition to writing and posting images to your Instagram blog. That said, you might like it!

THIS BOOK IS ABOUT BLOGGING AND ENGAGEMENT, REMEMBER?

We've learned how Instagram offers greater visibility to early adopters and that there are lots of visual content options and features available to Instagram users. Brands and individuals love to embrace new content creation tools because they help reach audiences and connect with them in new ways that set them apart from competitors.

It's fun to learn about the tools you have at your fingertips, but it's important to identify what and how you want to share. If you focus on writing your post, choosing a visual to go with it, and sharing to other channels to broaden your reach, you can always investigate other features as you forge your path blogging on Instagram.

BONUS: A REELS CONVERSATION WITH LORI MCNEE, ARTIST

Lori McNee @lorimcneeartist is an accomplished artist who lives and works in Sun Valley, Idaho. She has a large following on Twitter (100K) and 18.3K followers on Instagram. Besides being an artist, she's an author, teacher, blogger, and brand ambassador. Lori shares her art, processes, and life using Instagram posts, Instagram Reels, and Instagram Stories. As an early adopter of video formats, she saw increased visibility, engagement, and following. I asked her about how video has impacted her presence.

You've done a great job using Reels, Instagram Stories, and other video content on your feed. Does it require a lot of time, and is it worth it?

Lori: I've noticed a marked improvement in my Instagram account's growth since using Stories and Reels. I use the Stories to share a slice of my life each day. My audience likes seeing what I'm doing! Stories are a fun way for me to show my personality while building my brand.

I've had good luck since I started using Reels. It has been a powerful way to market my products, my art, promote my workshops, share ideas, and more.

I began using Reels shortly after they were first available. I tested the text overlay option, which I found interruptive, like I was yelling at my audience. Then I discovered a method where I staggered the content with the text overlays. The new approach was more discrete and worked well. I wanted to see how a call to action would work, so I included a CTA. It was very successful. I followed up with my "Peacock" Reels, and after a week, it had seventy-five thousand plays, which was pretty good for me!

Visuals are essential to artists like me, and my following is primarily from the fine art world. We love networking with other artists, discovering inspiring artists, as well as seeing artists demonstrate their secrets!

How frequently do you post Reels versus Stories or other videos, and have you noticed an appreciable difference in views, likes, and follows when using them?

Lori: One of the keys is consistency, especially with Reels. I'd see a more significant benefit if I posted more often. Frequency is especially valuable if I want my content to go viral. I would probably need to post one Reels a day, or at least one every other day. Instagram loves engagement and consistency. It wants you to be very active, and the algorithm will reward you! It treats you well when you post more frequently on the platform. It's also important to answer your comments and engage with your following. The combination of regular posting and engagement helps to push you to the top of the Explore page.

I've talked about hashtags in other parts of the book and wonder what you think about using them in a video?

Lori: I believe in the importance of using hashtags with Reels and even with Stories. I've found hashtags, like posts, work well with Reels. It's best to post hashtags in the caption section and keep them to thirty or less. You cannot edit Reels once they are posted, so it's best to first upload as a draft and then make edits there before you click "Share!" Also, music is a great addition to enhance both Reels and Stories. If you can find a song that's gone viral, try using that. Sometimes it helps!

How long does it take to create a Reels or Instagram Story, and how much time is spent in post-production before it's ready to share?

Lori: I am having fun creating the Reels, and they aren't that much work. I film some quick little videos while I'm painting. For example, I video an interesting painting tip or a section of my painting that's in progress. After my painting session, I put together my Reels. It takes anywhere between 20-60 minutes, depending on the complexity of the edits. It isn't difficult, but it's a bit tedious. I like finding music that enhances and relates to the video.

Stories are much simpler to create. You can use still photos or videos to create Stories. I love adding GIFs to my Stories to add personality. Reels and Stories can be fun and addicting to make! They're another art form and a great creative outlet. And just like with any art form, it takes practice to be good!

CHAPTER 11

FROM CAPTIONS TO CONTENT

———

IN THIS CHAPTER:

How Did Captions Become Content?

Longer Captions for Brands

Assessing Your Content

Your Content and the Explore Page

Insights Into Our Posts

Bonus: From Captions to Content

"Content is anything that adds value to the reader's life"

— *AVINASH KAUSHIK, AUTHOR AND*

DIGITAL MARKETING EVANGELIST

As I researched to see if there was data to support my ideas about extended captions and greater engagement, I noticed something: More people were blogging on Instagram.

Accounts with hundreds of followers and those with tens of thousands of followers were sharing blog-length updates. I observed that the longer posts, regardless of the account size, were earning increased interaction. Prior to 2016, the prevailing wisdom had always been to keep captions under 125 characters so they could be read in the feed without having to tap "more" (Jackson, 2020). It was fascinating to see so many people abandoning the accepted practice.

It was apparent that writers, whether individuals writing for themselves or content creators writing for brands, were the perfect candidates to take advantage of the 2,200-character storytelling space.

In 2019, when I started writing this book, the trend to longer posts had been quietly growing. One of the first articles I found describing the phenomenon, appeared in Repeller in 2017:

"I actually wouldn't call this a caption.
It's too long to be a caption! Too informative.
Too personal. You know what it reads more like?
A blog post. Yes, that's what I would call it —
a blog post, typed into the spot where an Instagram
caption usually goes. Lately, I've started to
wonder if Instagram is the new WordPress."

— HARLING ROSS, WRITER AND BRAND CONSULTANT

As a trend spotter, it wasn't surprising to see Ross among the earliest references. I continued my research for verified data as well as anecdotal evidence revealing insights about users who were sharing long-narrative posts.

HOW DID CAPTIONS BECOME CONTENT?

A 2019 study by social media analytics company, Quintly evaluated 5.4 million posts. They organized them into six groups arranged according to follower numbers. The study looked at growth rates, performance by type (image, video, or carousel), caption lengths, hashtags, emojis, and data based on when the posts were shared (Michalski, 2019).

Quintly's study showed that caption lengths have been increasing every year since 2016. By 2018, two-thirds of posts were longer than one hundred and fifty characters, and 36 percent of posts were using more than three hundred characters. That meant the majority of users on the platform were creating more extended captions. The findings aligned with my own experiences and observations.

The data revealed something significant: Influencers use Instagram to connect with their followers and communicate directly through their social media posts *instead* of writing blog posts. This finding was surprising and eye-opening!

> *"This year, Instagram captions are taking center stage on the platform."*
>
> —LATER.COM

Extended captions not only led to greater post engagement, but something else happened. It spawned a new kind of influencer: Instagram bloggers. This segment of users speaks to their audiences across niches, from health to beauty to spirituality to journaling and more. And they have been fostering huge communities by sharing authentic and relatable content.

I came across Instagram bloggers like Cleo Wade @cleowade (755K followers); Sarah Nicole Landry @thebirdspapaya (2 million followers); and Elise Darma @elisedarma (152K followers); who had taken Instagram, a visual platform, and flipped it on its head. Many Instagram bloggers with large audiences aren't household names, but they are well known to their followers. Their readers connect with them in the same way as you would connect with a friend. Astonishing numbers of readers engage with their updates. For example: A recent post by Landry gathered *120,000 likes* and *1,270 comments* in *twenty-four hours.*

I compared Landry's engagement as an Instagram blogger with a recent blog post by a legendary blogger, businessperson, and author. The top blogger's post had six comments after being "live" for five days, and no visible activity during the two weeks that followed. On the other hand, Landry's posts received a level of interaction you'd expect on the account of a bona fide celebrity. It's a clear illustration of how blogs may become less critical to marketing as social media channels offer greater functionality.

As the Instagram caption transformed into a blog post, it enabled Instagram bloggers to build engaged communities and broaden their reach into businesses, blogs, books, podcasts, and more.

LONGER CAPTIONS FOR BRANDS

Instagram users enjoy having direct connections with the people they come to know. I can say firsthand, I'm honored to know so many wonderful people on the platform. I know my book journey would've been much more difficult without their support and encouragement. At the end of this chapter, I share one user's experience in pursuit of engagement through extended posts.

Instagram users also enjoy having direct connections with brands they love. By using longer captions, brands have an opportunity to reveal more to their audiences and make them participants in the story. They can forge more connectedness through storytelling that resonates with readers.

If you're a writer seeking engagement on behalf of a brand, you can use longer captions to tell your brand's story in ways that provide value to your audience. Through content marketing, a brand's posts can provide insights into the brand's mission and products in ways that give meaning and drive more engagement, and ultimately more conversions.

In June of 2020, Vogue Magazine shared an Instagram post that received 45K+ likes and 190 comments. The post wasn't about fashion but instead showed how they understood and tapped into what matters to their audience. It showcased their support of Pride Month and featured a photo of Raquel Willis, a Black transgender activist, and writer. Along with an inspiring topic, it included excerpts from a Vogue feature, two tags, one hashtag, and a CTA, which linked to the extended story on Vogue's website:

> **@voguemagazine** (verified) "The charge for everyone this #Pride Month is to reflect on and restore the roots of the LGBTQ+ Movement," writes @raquel_willis. "Beyond pride campaigns and social media gestures, our fight was literally birthed from a collective that was multi-racial, gender-expansive, and anti-police brutality. And that fight goes beyond a few weeks each summer. The Black trans community has especially heeded the call recently with a rally drawing more than 15,000 people in honor of our lives and marches across the country. But the fight doesn't end here. You must make a lifelong commitment to ending the violence and discrimination that we face. After all, when Black transgender people are free, everyone else will also be free." (Vogue Magazine, 2021)

HubSpot notes that audience engagement is one way we can see content is reaching the right people and resonates with them. How do we meet objectives like increasing engagement by 10 percent or getting more traffic to a website? The answer is to share posts that provide value and relate well to your readers. When we're interested in our readers, we become more attractive to them. How can we tell if our content is reaching our audience? Diving into performance data will provide insights.

ASSESSING YOUR CONTENT

Many users may not have access to data, but the following section will provide some insights to give you an idea of how posts work, where users are, the best times to post, the lifespan of your post (how long it will continue to surface so people will find it in the feed), and how to access data and evaluate performance. If you find it valuable, it may be worthwhile to convert from a regular account to a business Instagram account.

Content Factoids

- In 2016, the average caption length was 142 characters (Later+Fohr, 2020).

- By 2018, the caption lengths crept up to 281 characters (Later+Fohr, 2020).

- In 2020, the projected caption length of 405 characters, which averages 65 to 70 words, was roughly 35 percent longer than captions from 2016 (Canning, 2020).

- In 2020, the average engagement rate across post types was 2.26 percent (Hubspot, 2021).

- The average lifespan of a post on Instagram is 48 hours — twice as long as Snapchat and 19 times longer than content on Facebook (Sonnenberg, 2020).

- The highest-performing posts on Instagram can take up to 12 hours to reach momentum (Sonnenberg, 2020).

- In 2021, the sweet spot for caption lengths are 500-1,000 and 1,000-2,000 characters (Hubspot, 2021).

YOUR CONTENT AND THE EXPLORE PAGE

Creating relevant content that engages your audience is one way for your post to land on the Explore page. The Explore page is Instagram's real-time recommendations system that shows you images based on what you like, save, share, and comment on. No two users will ever see the same results. On your feed, the algorithm shows you content shared by accounts you *already follow*, but on the Explore page, you'll see content from new accounts. More than half of Instagram users check out the Explore page each month.

The Explore page offers inspiration, relevancy, and discovery for everyone. When you share content that is likable and engaging (including comments from users and *your timely responses to them*), you could find your content featured there. It's exciting to have your content appear there because it means your post will be seen by new users who aren't already following you. (Those with business accounts can check post "insights" to see how many viewers find their posts on Explore.)

INSIGHTS INTO OUR POSTS

Instagram Insights is where you'll find data on your posts and it's available only to business or creator accounts.

It's necessary to connect your Instagram account to a related business Facebook Page to access Insights. I was curious, so I converted my personal account to a business account and found it a relatively simple process. I didn't have a business Facebook page, so I created one. I didn't want to have yet another social media property to maintain, but I created it just because I wanted to access the performance data on Instagram. Once I created and linked a business page, I could access the data and cross-post my Instagram content.

It will be valuable for you to convert your Instagram account and connect it to your business Facebook page. You may decide you'd like to run one of the ever-proliferating ads that users see on Instagram. The only way to do that is by having a connected Facebook page.

STEPS TO ACCESS DATA ON YOUR POST

There is a button beneath your bio on your home pages labeled "Insights." Tap it! Or another way to get there is in the upper right corner of your home page. Tap the "hamburger" menu, which is an icon that looks like three horizontal lines. When you take this route, you navigate to Insights and have access to other handy features, including YOUR activity. You can even set up a reminder here to make sure you're not spending too much time on Instagram!

- When you tap on Insights, you'll see a seven-day overview showing how many accounts you reached, the number of content interactions, and your total number of followers. You can tap the ">" symbol that appears next to each category of information to view specific metrics.

- Tapping "Accounts Reached" will take you to a screen that will show you the number of impressions (the number of times your post has been seen). The account activity you'll see will include how many profile visits, website taps, and if you have them, how many users tapped the buttons to email or call you.

- Similarly, by tapping "Content Interactions," you'll see the number of total interactions, post inter-actions (including likes, comments, and saves). If you posted an Instagram Story, IGTV post, or a Reels post, you'll see the actual numbers for each.

- If you posted an Instagram Story, the view count is available on the post and can be viewed for thirty days in Insights. Instagram Live broadcast counts restart after they're shared to IGTV and Reels.

- Tapping on "Followers" will take you to a break-down of your followers, showing overall numbers, the numbers of follows and unfollows, as well as where most are located, their ages, gender, and per-formance on given days. For example, if you click on "Fridays," you see the activity in three-hour increments. Note: Try not to obsess over unfollows!

FINDING INSIGHTS ON A SPECIFIC POST

For Insights on a specific post, navigate to the post you're interested in, and when it opens, tap "View Insights" under the picture. This will take you to the information about the post, including how many viewers your content reached; what percentage of accounts reached are NOT following you, and whether it was discovered from your "home," your "profile," from hashtags, via "Explore," or "other." Most views will likely be from "home."

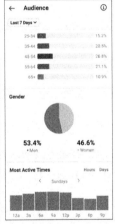

HOW INSIGHTS HELP

Insights tell us who interacts with our posts, including when and from where, and enable us to see which posts have been the most popular. When we see which image types are most successful, we can intentionally use them so more people will investigate our written content.

Insights show when your audience is most active. I post late at night on Fridays, which isn't optimum, and I know it reduces my visibility, but it's when I have time. When the algorithm deems your content to be relevant, it will show your post to more people. Recently, a long-time social media friend saw one of my photos and paused to check it out. She and I don't routinely interact, and she had no idea I'd been blogging on Instagram. It's an example of how disengaged users are less likely to see your content and how timing, content types, and engagement work together to help you.

Metrics can be useful as it helps users see the data beyond likes and comments. Viewing the number of people who visit your website, add your post to a collection (save it) or share to their Instagram Stories offers proof of what content most resonates.

BONUS: CAROL CUNNINGHAM: FROM CAPTIONS TO CONTENT

Carol Cunningham @i_likeit7 is a hobbyist photographer and an Instagram blogger who has 3K followers. She shares beautiful landscapes and photos from her adventures

and writes joyful posts peppered with emojis. I asked her about starting her account, her journey, and engagement on Instagram.

We had a family account, and I decided to go out on my own. When I did, only a few people followed me, so I had twenty to thirty followers when I started my account. A few months later, I had a post that jumped to four hundred likes (my average was just over one hundred.) I was desperate to find out why and came to realize some of the hashtags I used made it to the explore page for those hashtags.

One day in August 2017, I wrote a long, funny story about an adventure my husband and I had in Yosemite, CA. I had never written anything long before and really didn't think anyone would read it all. To my surprise, I had a huge response to the story! And many more personal comments beyond the regular, "nice shot" or "pretty pic," but real, what I'd call, connecting comments.

I thought it was a fluke, but I started to add a little more humor to my captions but kept them short. People seemed to like the humor, but the responses were still a bit shallow. I started to feel frustrated with IG, like I wasn't connecting the way I wanted to, and I thought a lot about the first time I had written a long caption and how well it seemed to connect with my IG friends.

I knew my photos were okay, but I also knew I needed something to make me different from every other account. So, sometime in 2018, I started writing longer captions with as much humor as possible. And yes, I believe it has made a difference! People seem to feel like they know me. I've even had people from other countries invite me to visit them when I'm traveling in their country! I truly believe the long captions and the humor was what brought about the connection. It's much, much, more work for me because I spend more time on the caption than I do on the editing of the photo, but it's been so worth it!

CHAPTER 12

MAKE YOUR FEED AWESOME

IN THIS CHAPTER:

Staying Inspired

Photos, Videos, and Other Image Types

Text as Art

Quotes as Art

Sources for Quotes

Stock Photography

Free and Amazing Resources

Image Resources

Low-cost Photos

Design and Content Tools

Web-based Applications

Mobile Apps

Rights Manager is Available on Instagram

Metadata

Should You Watermark Your Creations?

Watermark Apps

Are You Ready?

BONUS: Words as Images

"There are two distinct languages. There is the verbal, which separates people...and there is the visual that is understood by everybody."

— YAACOV AGAM, SCULPTOR

"Y ou talkin' to me?" Travis Bickle asked in the movie *Taxi Driver*. Our followers see content on their timelines and wonder the same thing—is a post talking to *them*?

Part of the challenge when we blog on Instagram is sharing an image that will attract eyeballs. Your viewers are your potential reading audience, so how do we get their attention?

When you first start on Instagram, it helps to share interesting, intriguing, attractive images because you're making your first impressions on your followers. When a post catches their eyes, and they stop to look, that's an opportunity to begin reading your captions. If your post adds value, and you invite them to participate, they'll respond.

Your Instagram feed doesn't need to be perfect right out of the gate. In fact, it would be unusual if it were! Scroll back to the beginning of anyone's Instagram, and you'll likely see how their content started and how it has changed over time. Some users settle into a personal style, and others don't. Having "no style" is a style in itself. Just keep in mind that as a writer, a good image is key. You need the visual that accompanies your post to draw attention to your writing.

This chapter is primarily a directory of resources to help people unsure about creating their images for their Instagram blogs. Many of these resources are great for other things, like creating a happy birthday Facebook post or artwork for craft projects. Websites come and go, but as of press time, the resources that follow are available to use, and many are free. A more extensive list of them is available in the Resource chapter of this book.

Some people share images from news stories (citing a link) because they're interested in topical subjects, and recognizable images attract the audience they want. Technology influencer, Chris Rauschnot, @24k, posts tech reviews, and shares videos of the products featured in his posts. Susan Palmer, @theguitarplayer, teaches guitar and uses photos and videos as visual content to go with her blog posts.

My images don't often reflect the content in my blog posts. Instead, I shoot photos to attract attention, then identify the contents at the end of my posts. Some users plan visuals to go with specific posts, and others share content created in the moment. However, all the examples we share have one goal in common—creating content and getting our audience's attention.

STAYING INSPIRED
Having a vision for your Instagram blog will help you maintain the momentum as it influences the look and feel of your grid. Your personal brand (Chapter 8) offers themes and grids to think about that can help define your personality. Having a preference about how you want your content to look is like having a road map to help you find your way.

"Photography is a great passion of mine. Over time my photos grow from what I see others do."

—FIONA @FIFI73DEE, INSTAGRAM USER

Even when you've settled on a path, it's good to continue watching and learning. Part of what inspires everyone on Instagram is the satisfaction of improving what we're doing and building new competencies. By discovering ways to ramp up your personal aesthetics, and seeing your gallery get better, you'll find it will attract more comments and interaction. It's a powerful motivator!

I've mentioned how I'll see opportunities and shoot photos wherever I am. By capturing them in the moment, I have them ready in my photo library. They're like insurance because if something better comes along, even the day of my post, I can go with it, but if not, I know I have something in my back pocket. It removes the concern about having a visual lined up. If you're doing something different, like posting quotes, gather up a dozen that you like and have them around for inspiration. Maybe one will tie-in to a new post topic or inspire you to write about one.

As for maintaining your motivation to write, the interaction you experience will be a positive reinforcer. However, writing can be hard work and having something difficult to do can lead to procrastination. Most of us know how fun *that* feels! (Not!)

One of the ways to keep yourself going is to develop a ritual. My Instagram is a weekly journal, so during the week I read my news feed or hear about events or developments going on my spheres of interest and make a note to myself to put it on my list of possible topics for my Instagram post. Sometimes I'll try to quickly rough out an idea and email it to myself, always prefacing the subject as "IG" so I know it relates to a possible post. Maybe it's just a topic or a topic with a couple of sentences, but it's enough to spur my memory. At some point on Friday, I will look at my ideas and choose something to flesh out. Sometimes I write a post and realize it's interesting only to ME, and I'll start over. I also think about possible hashtags when I'm composing, then take a quick peek in Instagram's "search" field to see what kind of traction different hashtags earn. There's more about hashtags in Chapter 9.

This is all to say, having a routine will go a long way to keeping you going. Comments and interaction will encourage you when you engage with your followers. You begin to make connections and a mutual interest develops, and you find yourself looking forward to their affirmations, responses, and engagement. When your followers are interested, it's a positive reinforcer that gives us further motivation.

PHOTOS, VIDEOS, AND OTHER IMAGE TYPES

If you choose to populate your feed *without* a camera and use "text as art," you'll find it's easy to turn text into your visual. By using a font, color palette, or certain style of frame around an image, you can establish a look and feel to your posts. The goal is to find an approach that resonates with your aesthetics and persona. If your content has a signature style, it will be recognizable when it surfaces in the feed.

When Instagram started in 2010, it was a photography platform, but after Facebook acquired it in 2012, Facebook added the ability to share videos (Del Gigante, 2013). The current quality of images on Instagram ranges from amateur to professional level. Users who post randomly for fun might not be concerned about the quality of their images, and that's OK because their images suit their purpose.

In addition to photos and videos discussed in Chapter 10, you'll also see nonpictorial content on Instagram. This chapter is focused more on content that doesn't require a camera.

With the general quality of images improving remarkably over the past decade, you hope your content will stand out among all the attractive images you see on Instagram. If you think your photos are nothing special, I encourage you to go back to tips in Chapters 6 and 9 and have fun learning ways to improve your images. You can also investigate apps that enhance what you're already doing. But if you think of yourself as noncreative, I have some options for you.

Instagram is a place for everyone—visual or not. These are solutions if you need to post an image with your blog post but lack confidence.

TEXT AS ART

An example of a successful Instagram blogger who shares text as art is Idil Ahmed (@idillionaire). Ahmed is the author of *Manifest Now,* and her combined presence on Twitter, Facebook, and Instagram numbers more than 1.27 million followers. She shares inspirational and uplifting blog posts with images that are simple screenshots of her quotes and excerpts. The engagement on her lengthy posts is other-worldly. Her text-as-art visuals prove that images aren't essential to be successful as an Instagram blogger.

Inspirational quotes are customizable to fit any account, whether business or personal, and exist to cover almost any topic. They can stand alone as words on a field of white or overlay colors, or you can pair them with background patterns or photos. Quotes are so well-liked that there are accounts solely dedicated to quotes as content. Some users write their own, and others use pre-made quotes that are available on the web. Some users utilize the image space as the space for their written posts. You'll find an example at the end of this chapter.

An account that does an amazing job of using text as art is @danpriceseattle. Dan Price is the CEO of Gravity Payments and has 133K followers. He uses text as art and blogs, thought-provoking news, information, and opinions that engage and ignite his audience. Most of his posts are black boxes with white text, branded with his name and avatar, and they're usually fewer than 50 words in length, making them easy to read. His signature style stops most people in their tracks. Thousands of his readers like his content, and hundreds actively participate in his posts through comments and questions.

QUOTES AS ART

Quotes can be a great option as a type of visual content. They're easy to make and can be inspiring, motivating, funny, or clever. No matter what you decide to write about in your blog post, finding an appropriate quote is possible. They're instantly consumable when they appear on the feed, and viewers often read and relate to them.

Finding a quote to go with your Instagram blog post is easy. Just enter the topics or keywords in your favorite search engine and check out the results. Ready-to-use quotes are convenient to use, but if you decide you want a uniform look, consider checking out some of the design resources below or listed in the Resource chapter.

Combining a quote with a beautiful image adds another layer of interest. A viewer who doesn't relate to a quote could be attracted to the photo used in the background. There are loads of free image sites available for you to use, or you can shoot a photo and combine it with a quote.

SOURCES FOR QUOTES
In addition to using a search engine, here are a couple of sources for inspirational quotes:

- **Goodreads** features thousands of searchable quotes that you can browse by tags: https://www.goodreads.com/quotes/tag/inspirational

- **QuotesGram** features copyright-free pre-made inspirational quotes: https://quotesgram.com/copyright-free-inspirational-quotes/

Once you start to investigate, you can find even more sources on the web.

STOCK PHOTOGRAPHY
If you can't shoot straight, or lack confidence in your artistic abilities, never fear—you have options. In fact, there are

many more than were available to graphic designers before everything went online. Before the web, designers, and art directors turned to companies such as Tony Stone, Corbis, and the Image Bank for high-end stock photography.

Since there was no "online," stock photo catalogs were the primary way to find stock images. In addition, purveyors designed, printed, and distributed hefty volumes of glossy perfect-bound books that featured photography from pros worldwide. In later years some included a companion CD, which was considered very "high tech!" With representatives worldwide, you could contact an office closest to you to license an image. It was a huge undertaking!

FREE AND AMAZING PHOTOS

In the early 2000s, disruptive stock photography options started to appear online. Getty was at the forefront of stock photography but was always an expensive proposition. In the past two decades, free photo sites have increased, and the quality of both free and inexpensive paid stock photos has improved.

You can find amazing images to share on Instagram to illustrate your posts. Again, you can enter keywords and see what kinds of ideas pop up. Remember how we talked about your brand and establishing a look and feel? When choosing photos, it makes sense to pay attention to the style of the pictures.

Some sites require attribution (giving credit to the photographer), and others don't. Even when credit isn't required, it's nice to attribute photos to the photographers who allow us to use their images for free. Some of the sites enable personal use, and others allow both personal and commercial use. Permissions vary, so it's essential to check when you find a photo you want to use.

I've assembled a list of free photo sites that are available as of mid-2021. Some have been around for a long time. For example, Morguefile began in 1996! Initially many sites didn't include the ability to search. In the days before artificial intelligence, tagging an image with keywords was a laborious process, usually for the person or people uploading the photos. Now many of the resources are searchable. In addition, there are surprising options available if you have a particular content idea in mind.

IMAGE RESOURCES

Creative Commons is a nonprofit that works worldwide to help enable sharing of creative properties for the public to use (Creative Commons, 2021). There are different levels of permission, and they're cited on each site. Public Domain licensing is designated with "(CC0)." On the lists, other features are noted, such as search features or if images on the site are free to use without license or crediting the photographer.

In the back of this book, the Resource chapter lists more tools. Here are a few of the sites that I've used in recent years.

- **Unsplash** (searchable; Unsplash license) https://unsplash.com/ — Unsplash is the first site I go to when I need to find a free stock photo. It's easy to use and has a nice selection of photos that reflect the photographers who shoot them. In other words, you might find more conceptual images here and a greater variety of styles. In March 2021, Getty Images acquired

Unsplash. (Surprise!) As of mid-2021, images use the Unsplash license as opposed to CC0, and continues to operate as it did prior to the Getty acquisition (Cho, 2021). Attribution isn't required, but photographers appreciate it when they receive credit for their work.

- **Pexels** (searchable; CC0) https://www.pexels.com/ — Pexels is a site I'd sometimes use when I needed a small, generic healthcare image, but it has myriad categories encompassing photos and video that you can search for by topic. Pexels has a cool option for searching by color, concept, mood and even includes flatlays (images shot from a bird's-eye view) where you can superimpose text. Attribution isn't required, but it's appreciated!

- **Pixabay** (searchable, CC0) https://pixabay.com/ The site offers royalty-free stock photos, illustrations, vector images, videos, and music that are free to use commercially and without attribution. The content is offered "as is" and is not warranted. It accepts no liability for use except as described in its license. You can learn more about their terms on their website.

LOW-COST PHOTOS

Is there an advantage to paying for a photo when a similar photo can be found on a free site? Since free photos are, well, *free*, there's a good chance an image will be used by multiple customers. For projects with small budgets, I have used iStockphotos (acquired by Getty in 2006), Shutterstock, and others, and purchased images for reasonable fees. You can check across the sites listed in the Resources section to view their offerings and compare prices.

DESIGN AND CONTENT TOOLS

Are you intrigued to try building quotes or composite (type and image) graphics? There are lots of applications and services that make it easy to do. Some are web-based (to use on your computer), and some are apps available for iPhone or Android devices. Some are free, and others offer free versions with optional in-app purchases (where you pay to access premium features). There are also paid apps that offer free trials, so you can try before buying or paying for a subscription.

From the days of Aldus PageMaker to the advent of Adobe Creative Cloud apps, graphic design hasn't always been easy for the average person. But try telling that to someone who uses Canva! With Canva, it's easy to create content that reflects you and your brand. I started using it in 2021 to create digital content for the web. I was impressed because it's easy to use and offers a surprising number of options. I decided to pay for a subscription. It can do a faster and more accurate "image outline" than I can make in Photoshop! I wouldn't use it for traditional print, though. I routinely use X-Y coordinates to precisely place an element in a specific location or optically kern type (adjust the spacing between letters). Granular control isn't its strong suit.

For Instagram and other users, it's super flexible. I love how @barbiesartgallery uses colors, fonts, and elements in Canva to create recognizable content for her feed.

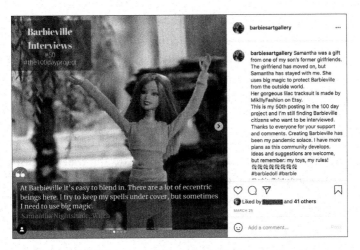

There are many fun elements in each of @barbiesartgallery's posts, including titles, graphic inset quotes, and colored bars.

WEB-BASED APPLICATIONS

Since I'm not a kid, I like the real-estate of a full screen, mouse, and keyboard. So here are a few web-based applications to check out (you'll find more in the Resource chapter in the back of the book).

- **Adobe Spark**

  https://spark.adobe.com/ —My favorite free web-based application is Adobe Spark. I've used it to create videos, graphics, and presentations. You can take a variety of components (images, videos, text overlays, full frames of text) and add music, too. It's quite awesome!

- **Canva**

  https://www.canva.com/ iOS, Android, or web —I began using Canva with my Indiegogo crowdsource campaign that helped fund this book! The thing that stood out the most (besides being easy to use) was the ability to iterate and keep copies of content updates across Twitter, Instagram, Facebook, Facebook Groups, and LinkedIn. Each content type has dimensions that work best, and the templates built into the app are great.

- **Tyle.io**
  https://tyle.io/ —Tyle.io is a nifty little app that you can use to create noticeable and optimized video content quickly and easily.

MOBILE APPS

If you're using iOS 10 or later, you can use the iPhone Markup editor on your iPhone or iPad to play around with ways of combining photos and quotes. Here are two popular mobile apps to use for creating quote content.

- **Crello**—iOS, Android (also on the web!) lets users easily create designs and animations. You can use one of their templates or build from scratch.

- **Text 2 Pic**—iOS, Android—You can choose from dozens of text styles, effects, and colors, access thousands of free stock photos from Pixabay. You can also use built-in filters to style your images.

- **Werble**—iOS—Similar to Tyle, Werble does some pretty cool animations. I recently began following someone on Instagram who uses it and can't help but notice his content.

IMAGE EDITING APPS

- **Snapseed**—iOS, Android—This is my favorite all-around image editing app. It lets users correct imperfections, sharpen, adjust curves, expand, correct perspective, and perform myriad adjustments to their photos. You can then apply filters using built-in presets or create your own combinations. I love this app.

- **Prisma**—iOS, Android—This is a fascinating image editing app that uses artificial intelligence and neural networks to transform photos into works of art. You can choose a genuinely boring photo and turn it into something exciting and beautiful. There are tons of filter styles, and to access more, you can pay for access through in-app purchases. I truly love this app!

There are vast numbers of photo editing and design apps on iPhone, Android, or the web. You might discover some on your own. You can jot them down here unless you're reading an ebook or library copy!

_____

_____

_____

_____

_____

_____

RIGHTS MANAGER IS AVAILABLE ON INSTAGRAM

The Facebook Rights Manager helps content creators protect their images and videos across Instagram and Facebook and provides tools for creators (who are often also the rights owners), so they can report intellectual property (IP) violations.

The Facebook Rights Manager is designed for people or businesses seeking control over how, when, and where their content is shared across Instagram and Facebook. The tool cross-references uploaded content across Facebook's platforms and notifies owners of possible violations. It protects publishers and creators that regularly publish significant volumes of content that viewers love to share. If you're interested in this feature, you must submit an application to request access to Rights Manager. You can choose videos or images (or both).

METADATA

Metadata is invisible data that can include the author, when the image was created or modified, the file size, and the type of device used to take a photo. You can protect your photos by inserting metadata in your pictures using an application such as Adobe Photoshop or Lightroom. More often, users concerned about their photos being "stolen" (used without permission) watermark or identify their images with their names or Instagram monikers.

SHOULD YOU WATERMARK YOUR CREATIONS?

To watermark or not to watermark? Some users feel better adding a copyright © with their names on their images, but Instagram doesn't like it. For example, suppose you're creating art for a quote. In that case, you can copyright it *only* if you made the quote and all of the elements that went into it (the words, the background image, or other details). If you don't own everything in your creation, you don't have the right to watermark it.

WATERMARK APPS FOR ANDROID AND IPHONE

If you want to watermark original content wholly created by you, there are apps for that! Note that adding copyright will not completely protect you from infringement, but it instills a sense of security for some users. For example, you will notice across Instagram users who superimpose their names, sometimes with a © copyright symbol.

I don't watermark my photos, but here are a few apps that were recently reviewed and recommended (Elink, 2020):

- **iWatermark** (iOS and Android)

- **Watermark X** (iOS)

- **Add Watermark on Photos** (Android)

There are additional apps listed in the Resource chapter.

ARE YOU READY?

I hope so! I've tried dozens of apps over the past decade, and most have been deleted. However, the "sticky" ones prove to be useful, versatile, and easy to use. That's why some of the best ones have been around for a long time.

There are tons of apps on every platform. Some are just plain fun, and others more than pull their weight. Applications both on the web and for mobile devices can help us build a visual presence on Instagram and create content for other channels.

I encourage you to investigate what's out there. You might discover the perfect app to help you create awesome content that reflects who you are and help you establish your brand on Instagram.

BONUS: WORDS AS IMAGES

Nancy Ayenajeh @dnacelo_ is a Nigerian writer who started blogging on Instagram in November 2020. She has 2,160 devoted fans who read and engage with her content. Her grid includes personal photos and carousels of 2-9 slides of her writing, quotes, and poetry.

My journey on Instagram got off on a rocky start. I'm an introvert and a shy person, and at first, I didn't know how to connect with readers. I was struggling to express myself, and it was frustrating. This went on and on to the point that I almost gave up... until one day, I felt some motivation. I encouraged myself not to quit and continue doing what I was doing. I took my advice and decided to just go with the flow to see what happens. The rest was history. I chose Instagram to share my writings because it is the social media app where my strength lies, and it is where I can connect with people and share my stories. It is a platform that is easier for me to use and luckily, this is where my target readers are found.

Three posts on Nancy's feed. The center post with the double squares in the upper right indicate it's a carousel post. Nancy will often have as many as 9 slides in a carousel. The slides are easily swiped to the left, revealing more text.

CHAPTER 13

ARE YOU FEELING LUCKY?

IN THIS CHAPTER

There is No 13th Chapter

"Luck Is What Happens When
Preparation Meets Opportunity"

— SENECA

THERE IS NO 13TH CHAPTER

I had a weird feeling about wrapping up my book on Chapter 13. It's not that I have triskaidekaphobia, but why take a chance by ending on an unlucky number?

In the hope of avoiding bad karma, I've written this as a nod to *Wayside School is Falling Down* by Louis Sachar—a book we read to our sons, Andrew and Charley, when they were young. If we're lucky, maybe we'll read it to our grandchildren one day.

In *Wayside School*, there was no 19th floor (Sachar, 1989).

In *Blogging on Instagram*, there is no 13th Chapter.

CHAPTER 14

TIPS FOR BUILDING COMMUNITY

IN THIS CHAPTER:

First Things First: Facebook and Contacts

Ways to Grow

Follower Tactics

Hashtags

Active Engagers

Fakes and Bots

Organic Engagement

Essential Interaction

Close Friends

Content as Catalyst

Don't Obsess about Follower Numbers

Creating Real Experiences

BONUS: Growth Strategies from Real People

"People forge bonds in places that have healthy social infrastructures—not because they set out to build community, but because when people engage in sustained, recurrent interaction, particularly while doing things they enjoy, relationships inevitably grow."

—ERIC KLINENBERG, AUTHOR

New and experienced users have asked the same question: "How do you grow your followers on Instagram?"

This chapter is packed with a lot of information gleaned from personal experience, interviews, and research. On the Internet, the same recommendations appear repeatedly, so I've included the standard stuff and tapped into insights from actual users. So, read through and see what looks interesting or possible for your account.

In *"2021 on Instagram: What do the numbers say?"*—a report by HubSpot and Mention—many findings reinforce prevailing wisdom. Based on the analysis of 100 million posts representing two million users, it found caption lengths getting the most significant engagement have 500 to 1,000 and 1,000 to 2,000 characters, which translate to anywhere from roughly 100 to 300 words.

Longer posts and storytelling boost organic follower growth, but you increase the chances to grow your audience by following some basic suggestions:

- Complete your bio, including keywords.

- Create Stories highlights if you have a business account (they're circles with labels along the top of a business account where Instagram Stories are archived).

- Consistently post high-quality content.

- Interact with your community, and that means replying to comments and direct messages and responding to tags.

- Mix up your content with images, videos, Stories, IGTV, and Reels (Hubspot and Mention, 2021).

FIRST THINGS FIRST

The easiest way to kick start your Instagram audience is to follow your Facebook friends. They're the most likely to follow you back.

- Just log in to Instagram and tap the hamburger menu (it looks like three horizontal lines in the upper right), and then tap on "Discover people." The first choice you see should be, "Connect to Facebook."

- Under "All Suggestions" is a list of users you're friends with on Facebook. Tap the "follow" button next to the accounts you want to connect!

Similarly, you can sync the contacts on your device to Instagram, which will recommend accounts to follow. (Note, if your plumber has an Instagram account, it's possible he/she would be recommended to you!) Once again, tap the hamburger menu, then:

- Tap Settings
- Tap Account
- Tap Contact Syncing, then Connect Contacts

Based on your contacts, Instagram will recommend accounts for you to follow when you've completed the sync setup. The list syncs periodically, and you can delete your synced contacts if you ever change your mind by heading back to your Account, Contact Syncing, and turning it off. You might also see a list of "Suggested" accounts, listing people who are new to Instagram. They might not have many followers yet, so if you decide to follow them, you could be among the first to discover their content.

Once you've followed a few dozen people, chances are you'll soon have some followers whose posts will populate your feed.

Your *actions* influence the posts that show up on your feed. The Instagram algorithm pays attention to the people you follow, the kinds of content they share, and the posts you share, like, save, and engage with. If you're following a small number of people, chances are you'll be able to see almost everything posted. In 2021, you're allowed to follow a maximum of 100-150 accounts (in addition to those you already follow) per day (Social Pros, 2021).

WAYS TO GROW

FOLLOW FOR FOLLOW
Using the "Follow for Follow" method of growing your following, you follow as many accounts as possible, with the expectation that a percentage will follow back.

An informal test took place in 2020 where one hundred accounts were followed; one hundred accounts were followed plus content was liked; and the final one hundred accounts received a follow, like, and comment. The results show this tactic is still working:

- Follow only—Follow back rate: 14 percent
- Follow with a like—Follow back rate: 22 percent
- Follow with a like and comment—Follow back rate: 34 percent (MacDonald, 2020).

Businesses have content creators and strategists on staff, but who has time to vet individuals when building an audience? For businesses, it's easy to check their competitors and follow and engage with their audiences. For individual users, check out followers of trusted accounts.

CURATED FOLLOW FOR FOLLOW

I like to curate additions to my community because I want to connect with real, relatable people who are active and share content I like. You can choose an account you're following where you enjoy the content and engagement, then tap on the list of their followers (the most recent will be at the top). You can check out bios and content, and if you see someone you want to add to your community, follow them, like a few photos and leave a comment.

A variation is to look at comments left on posts you see. If you notice a recent comment, there's a chance they're still active. You can like the comment and leave a response, then go to the account, like a few things and comment, then follow.

FOLLOW/UNFOLLOW

Follow/Unfollow is a growth hack used by accounts that are only interested in numbers. It's different than Follow for Follow because engagement isn't a goal—the only objective is to gain followers. Users follow a ton of accounts, and if they aren't followed back in a few days, they unfollow them. Even if they ARE followed back, in a few days, they *still* unfollow. In other words, followers are dumped no matter what. This method, which is very numbers driven and not very people-driven, apparently still works (Aigrow, 2021).

SEARCH FOR HASHTAGS

There have been a few references to hashtags throughout the book. For the most comprehensive explanation, check out Chapter 9. Hashtags are great for attracting people to the topics you are sharing and make it easy to find what you're interested in. If you go to "search" and type in a hashtag or topic that reflects your interests, you may discover accounts you want to follow. You can follow and hope for a follow back but may have better luck if you follow, like, and comment. Smaller accounts are more inclined to follow back.

NOTICE ACTIVE ENGAGERS

If you notice people who like and leave comments on the content of those you follow, and the content falls into the same niche as yours, click on the commenter's avatar and check out their feed. Maybe this is someone who would also enjoy *your* content, so go ahead and follow them. When you like several of their images in sequence, or like an image and post a comment, they're alerted. A sequence of "likes" is sometimes noticed, but a mention is hard to miss and often opens the door for engagement.

WATCH OUT FOR FAKES!

For every social media platform, there are services that sell fake followers. For example, click farms create massive amounts of fake/spam accounts that are sold to anyone who wants to make their account followings look larger or look more active than they are. Unfortunately, inexperienced users don't always recognize fake accounts. In some cases, a legitimate account follows one of the fake ones. In that case, they inadvertently lend legitimacy because friends see them following an account and assume it must be OK. So be on the lookout for:

- Private accounts, where you can't see the kind of content they post
- An account that was recently created and follows tons of accounts
- Incomplete or generic profile descriptions and nonsensical bios with typos
- Nonfunctional links on their bios
- Only one photo on their grid
- No captions on their posts
- No likes or comments on their posts
- Tons of images of the same person in variations of a pose
- Guys with lots of pictures of themselves in surgical garb, military uniforms, or dressed as pilots
- Extremely unbalanced follow ratios (e.g., they follow 2,000 people and have three followers)
- No engagement on their content

Bots and fake accounts can influence opinions. Maybe you saw it depicted in Season 7 of *Homeland*! Fraudulent accounts can be set up to follow users for questionable reasons, such as the "men" who prey on vulnerable and lonely women or the reverse—women who look to prey on lonely men.

Buying followers, likes, and comments to make your account look popular is not a good strategy. Some think that the more fans and followers they have make them seem cooler or more important. Social platforms like Twitter and Instagram periodically go through and clear out fake followers. This means that accounts that inflate their popularity by buying artificial followers will experience a drop in followers and then must reinvest the money to maintain the illusion. Don't be tempted to buy your way to the top.

Engagement is the holy grail of brand awareness on Instagram. Vanity metrics like follower counts matter to many users, but they don't measure engagement rates (Roach, 2021). The more diverse your content, the more chances you will have to have to reach and interact with your audience.

Users deploy tools and apps to automatically follow and unfollow people when they aren't followed back. There are also apps and services that will like content. The caveat here is Instagram doesn't want people to use automation or apps to grow their followings or to inflate engagement rates. Apps can be banned, and accounts using them can be punished. Instagram algorithms pick up on the unusual activity and discourage users by disabling their accounts. Real people who rapidly like and comment on posts are in danger of being put into the Instagram "time out corner" because their activity looks "bot-like."

BOTS

Users appreciate meaningful and relevant comments, but even a short comment can lead to back-and-forth conversations.

There are bots that fake engagement by automatically following, liking, and commenting on posts under the guise that it's *you*. Hootsuite experimented and found several problems with automation, including:

- People don't like bots and can tell when something is fake.

- Instagram actively works against activity that debases the experiences of users (Cooper, 2021).

GROW THROUGH ORGANIC ENGAGEMENT

A best practice is to let your account grow naturally through organic following and engagement. Most importantly, the process should be fun, because if you enjoy it, you'll stick with it. And if you stick with it, you'll succeed. In a recent post, marketing platform, Later, lists eleven ways to increase engagement in 2021:

1. Discover your best time to post (go to Insights > Audience, to see best days and times).
2. Start conversations with Instagram Stories stickers.
3. Regularly test and analyze new content types.
4. Create "savable" content for your feed.
5. Share data your audience will love.
6. Write longer captions.
7. Open up about your brand and business.
8. Add an element of fun.
9. Pay closer attention to your hashtags.

10. Create shareable content.
11. Create more video content (Canning, 2021).

Two additional actions that can help include:

- Pay for a sponsored post.
- Make sure your post is geotagged.

ESSENTIAL INTERACTION

If you're new to Instagram, it might feel weird to "like" or comment on photos or blog posts that have been shared by people you don't know ... yet. However, when you share a post and people respond by liking, commenting, saving, or sharing it, it's gratifying, and we all value that experience. When you reach out, others reach back to you.

Viewing and liking other people's content is essential, especially in the beginning. It's the first step in creating relationships. Your interactions increase the odds of having your content shown to more people. Instagram interprets two-way interaction as a signal of a connection or preference.

After connecting with Facebook and other friends, you can add some entertainment value to your feed by searching for and following brands or celebrities but be aware: they rarely follow back or engage. However, suppose you create user-generated content (UGC is content that supports or amplifies a product or brand) and tag the account. In that case, there's a chance brands and celebrities *will* engage with you. For example, I remember tagging Google in a post during CES2019 (the 2019 Consumer Electronics

Show). When Google liked my post and made a comment on my feed, my post made it to the Explore page, and I was thrilled!

CLOSE FRIENDS

Close Friends is a subset of followers that have access to private Instagram Stories that are distributed only to close friends. For me, Close Friends also represents a special group of people I want to remember for a variety of reasons.

Reciprocal interaction enables users to see each other's posts on the feed. The absence of interaction means content can disappear from the feed. To see what a friend has posted, it necessitates going to their page to catch up with their content. I have a long-time Twitter friend who is also on Instagram, and we noticed neither of us ever saw each other's posts. So, we set about visiting each other's feeds and liking and commenting on a bunch of content. It did the trick because our content began to show up in one another's feeds.

You can add people to your "Close friends." I use it as a bookmark for people I like, and it makes it easy to navigate to their Instagram pages and see what they're doing. Instagram, for some reason, doesn't always show you what your close friends are posting, which is odd since it would seem logical that you'd want to see their content. But no-o-o-o. Instagram thinks it knows what you will like! By the way, no one knows if they're on your close friends list, so no one knows if they're removed. If content shared by some of your favorite people isn't surfacing in your feed, the close friends list is a great shortcut for keeping tabs on people you care about.

USE CONTENT AS A CATALYST

Bloggers on Instagram receive some of the most engaging comments because their posts invite interaction. If you take a moment to compliment someone, they usually reply. In time, you could find yourself with a new friend in Sweden, a virtual "sister" in Brisbane, or a new friend in the Arctic Circle. It's incredible how relationships form through posts, comments, and responses. In 2019, Instagram friends from the UK, California, Hawaii, and other parts of the US came to Seattle, and I met them in real life, all because of Instagram.

DON'T OBSESS ABOUT FOLLOWER NUMBERS

By allowing your account to grow slowly, you'll have more opportunities to get to know your community. You'll discover ordinary, down-to-earth folks who aren't that different from you. They care about some of the same things you care about and experience the same kinds of life events. We've all lived through a pandemic, social and political events, happenings in the economy, and personal triumphs or losses. There is a reason why 53 percent of accounts have fewer than 1,000 followers—many users enjoy knowing and even bonding with the people in their audiences, and it's easier for that to happen when your account is a manageable size.

CREATING REAL EXPERIENCES

In 2008 I jumped into social media because a client, Aaron Blank, owner and CEO of the Fearey Group in Seattle, started using Twitter and said, "Terri, you need to check this out." At the time, social media was shiny and new, and I was skeptical. Nevertheless, I found that Twitter was a welcome contrast to the sometimes-creepy chat rooms on AOL. There was something profoundly exciting about participating in a global conversation with your neighbors in Europe, Asia, and different parts of the world. Real-time conversations were intoxicating.

The same sensation happens on Instagram. It's alive 24-hours a day, every day of the year. I've often thought how, because of social media, there is no reason for loneliness.

Maybe you've participated in Facebook to stay in touch with family, or LinkedIn to build your professional network. Suppose you have a yearning to write and love taking or viewing photos. In that case, Instagram offers an opportunity to write for your own reasons, in your own time frame, and to build and participate in a community of people who become part of your life.

I asked my followers what they did before social media because it has become such a presence in our lives. Several said they used to watch a lot more TV. It's fun to see your IG feed instead of channel surfing. Sometimes I'll see a post that is so incredibly beautiful it stops me in my tracks. Other times I'll see an image and wonder how a certain look was achieved, and it inspires me to try something new. Of course, spending time on Instagram and interacting with your community will help your images reach a wider audience. Still, another great benefit of viewing and engaging, and one of the most valuable, is how it expands your view of the world.

If you've read this far, you now have some ideas about using Instagram for blogging. You have access to helpful tools and resources to enhance your experiences, and you have an idea of how to start building your community of friends and followers on Instagram.

In 2020, there was an unprecedented confluence of events, including the coronavirus pandemic, the Black Lives Matter movement to address and correct social injustices, and catastrophic outcomes that resulted from climate change. COVID-19 thrust many of us into isolation, making it more important to connect with others. Instagram, in many ways, filled that void. By sharing on Instagram and building a community there, we discover just how small the world is. Shared experiences across time zones, countries, and languages have shown how we have much more in common with each other than we ever imagined.

It's exciting to get to this part of the book because it means you're prepared to take the plunge! Take your time to experiment with your visual and written content and experience how it feels to publish your posts. If you find me and follow @terrinakamura, post a reply and I will follow you back. I would love to check out what you're writing and maybe even leave one of your first comments.

Please say hello and introduce yourself and use the hashtag #NowBOI (Now Blogging on Instagram) so I can find your posts. I'll do my best to answer any questions you might have, and I'll look forward to making your acquaintance on Instagram.

BONUS: GROWTH STRATEGIES FROM REAL PEOPLE

Terri Nakamura @terrinakamura, 8.2K followers

For pure enjoyment, share what you like, and like what is shared with you. There are gimmicky ways to get likes and follows by sharing viral memes and the hashtags that go with them, but I've always shared original content. A few years ago, I tried to grow my following because I wanted access to extra features that were available only to those with 10K+ followers. I gave up because I had no time, but back then, I looked at people whose content was similar to mine, then reviewed their followers to find people whose content interested me. When I found an active account with great content, I'd follow them, like a few of their photos, and leave a comment or question on one of their posts, and often I'd be followed back.

Lori McNee, @lorimcneeartist, 18.3K followers

I have slowed down on my posting because it takes time to prepare good-quality content. I don't think it has affected my growth. I have noticed Reels have helped me grow faster than anything else! I wish I had time to make them more frequently because they are fun! My advice is to find your own voice. Understand your niche to help grow your audience. Use hashtags that are relevant to your niche and find some that reach beyond it. Mix them up. Answer comments. Engage with other accounts. Time your postings to reach your target audience. For instance, 9:20 a.m. PST is a good time for me to post a Reel.

Pat Weaver, @webgrrrrl, 4.3K followers

I don't use the explore page much. If I've ever appeared on it, I don't know about it. I think most of my new followers probably find me via hashtags. I'm choosy about hashtags, avoiding those with millions of posts. If they're that busy, I figure my posts will get lost there. Ditto the very small ones: if they aren't being used, nobody's looking at them. So, I tend to go in for those with between 20k and 150k. I was curious and started a hashtag of my own not too long ago. I think it hasn't been around long enough actually to get any notice, though. So, most of my new followers find me via hashtags and by noticing comments I've left on other people's posts.

Imei Hsu, @myallergyadvocate, 800 followers

I try to post daily, but life happens. I wax and wane followers based on my post frequency, losing five to ten if I don't post once a week. My advice to someone new is to grow your following organically versus purchasing followers, and engage with followers with good content, showing care and kindness in your posts.

Nancy Ayenajeh, @dnacelo_, 2.2K followers

I didn't take the usual route of connecting Facebook friends. It took me almost a month to reach 1,000 followers. To build my following, I just:

- Chose the right media platform,

- Decided on the kind of content I wanted to post,

- Became consistent with my posts using the right hashtags and,

- Engaged with my audience whenever they or I put up a post

Jack Higgins, @jackandpele, 1.4K followers

Whether you are writing a novel, an article, blogging, or Instagramming, the way to attract a following is to get the reader emotionally attached to your message. Pretend you are talking to a friend. Over time my readers become friends, and it sometimes leads to making them part of my narrative. Being included in my posts makes them part of an exclusive club, and if they're willing to share the secret, they tell others about it. I can't say this is a repeatable tactic, but I now have an inner circle of approximately one hundred people—quite a number of people that form a unique community.

Kate Terra @kate.terra, 3.5K followers

My advice to a new account: You have to put in the time to engage with other people to get the most out of Instagram. Exploring hashtags, sharing, engaging with stories, and commenting on posts not only drives up your numbers but also makes Instagram more fun and rewarding!

Evgenia Zaslavskaia, @zaslavskaia__evgenia, 13.4K followers

I am often asked this question. You need to follow many people because they follow in response. This is necessary because for five hundred people you'll find approximately one interesting, witty person. I used to do that, and now I know two dozen wonderful people. Of course, there are a lot of witty and smart people, but they don't show up on Instagram. And the second tip: new bloggers should not pointlessly write comments to posts "delicious and beautiful," but instead, express their thoughts. If more people would do this, Instagram would be much more enjoyable.

Carol Cunningham, @i_likeit7, 3.1K followers

I found that if a big account featured me, I would get more followers. One prominent account featured me, and I got over 1,000 likes, and I acquired quite a few new followers. After that, I started following more accounts that posted my kind of photos. If the account was small, I had a better chance of being featured, but the impact on my account was barely noticeable. But if more than one small account featured the same picture, then that would give me noticeable traffic. Another thing I've done is search to find recent posts, then like, comment, or follow.

Diana Horsfall, @queenhorsfall, 53K followers

When I began on Instagram, I used an iPhone to shoot photos, but a follower advised me to buy a real camera, so I did. I learned photography and Adobe Lightroom and had good instincts about fashion and styling photos, so my account attracted the attention of brands, and I became a fashion influencer. I attribute some of my account growth to sponsorships and collaborations. I collaborated with major brands such as Coach, Fossil, Victoria's Secret, Macy's, and others. The brands were tagged in my posts, so people interested in the brands often saw my content. Other things that drew attention were the promotions and giveaways that I featured in my posts. They proved to be very effective for attracting followers.

Emelina Spinelli, @ecspinelli, 65.2K followers

Instagram has come down on gamification, so tactics like Follow/Unfollow aren't as easy or as effective. I often encourage clients to think of writing captions as short blog pieces, but in addition, here are five ideas I recommend for small accounts to grow:

- Focus on video content because it keeps people on their platform longer.

- Make sure that you are tagging yourself and your account in your video posts, so viewers have a way to find your account.

- Use between five and ten, super-targeted hashtags, with between 50 and 400,000 results. Make sure the hashtags are extraordinarily relevant to your content. The Instagram AI can detect what's in your photo and vet against the hashtags.

- Start advertising your posts, selecting an "automatic audience," where your image (ad) is shown to people who have demographic and psychographic similarities to your current base.

- Encourage your audience to both share and save your content. Instagram introduced a feature where you can share other people's posts on your Stories. There's a clickable feature that lets viewers read and follow (*Emelina Spinelli*, 2020).

Sebastian Juhola, @theminimalistwardrobe, 229K followers

The first thing I started doing was contacting accounts of the same size (or smaller), asking them to do a shoutout exchange with The Minimalist Wardrobe. After that, they'd simply post about me, and I'd post about them.

I spent hours and hours finding suitable accounts to cross-promote with, and I must've sent over a hundred DMs daily to people. I didn't mind if the accounts were smaller. Anything over one thousand was worth it for me, as posting was easy, and my audience seemed to enjoy the posts.

Once I grew, I could get bigger accounts on board, which is why the growth was exponential. I had also perfected my strategy by only contacting accounts with good engagement and instructing them on how to promote The Minimalist Wardrobe when agreeing on the shoutouts. A clear call-to-action to follow made a huge difference (Juhola, 2020).

Henie Reisinger, @heniereisinger, 30.8K followers

For me, IG is my personal haven. Through the years, I have garnered friends and followers because there is mutual respect for nurturing each other. We post for no other reason than we enjoy each other and share authentically. It's not about increasing likes, comments, or followers. It's about a shared community of kindness and support for each other. I have many IG friends from all over the world, and I cherish each one! There is no shortcut for sharing love, peace, and joy! You reap what you sow!

Andrew Sears, @alterediis, 37K followers

Posting once a day is extremely crucial on any social media platform for long-term growth. However, the more your followers know about you, the more important you become to them, so when you're building a page, work to create one-on-one relationships with your audience. For bloggers, if you want to grow on Instagram, you'll need to learn the visual part of the platform and understand what's appealing. Heck, you don't even need to share your own photos—you can find something on the Internet. When I was starting, I didn't have a $2,000 camera, but I could go on the Internet and find images that were royalty-free. I tag artists if I share their work to my page so people can look them up, and the artists benefit, too. You need to create a visually appealing grid, so viewers come to your profile and say, "This is a blogger? I love these images."

ACKNOWLEDGEMENTS

Some of you might have noticed I made a few movie references in this book. Some of the films aren't even favorites, but they served my purposes! I'd like you to think of this section as the credits that roll at the end of a film. I don't know about you, but I always watch to the end. I never know what I'll see.

First, I'd like to thank Georgetown professor Eric Koester, who sent me a note on LinkedIn in January 2020 asking me if I was interested in writing a book. I was! I joined his program through Creators Institute and New Degree Press, and it changed my life.

My Indiegogo supporters are real heroes who made this book possible. Family, friends, strangers, and fellow authors rallied to help. I have profound gratitude for their belief in me. Thank you:

Cynthia & Carl Asai	Roger Beaty
Kyle Barber	Julia B-Bende
Putnam Barber	Judy Bequette
Leo Basic	Lynne Berry

Rex Bobbish

MA & Rick Boggs

Jamie Bosse

Sue Brush

George Bryant

Emma Burnham

Charles & Gwendoline
Coolidge

Eunice Corbin

Linda Criddle

Susan Cummings

Suzanne Cushing

Soren Dalsgaard

George David

Georgiana Dearing

Frank Denman

Deborah Finch

Zia Gipson

Jennifer Good

Shauna Groenewold

Charmaine & Bill
Hartshorn

Claudia Heredia &
Luis Pilco

Jack & Nancy Higgins

Andrew & Diana Horsfall

Charles M. Horsfall

David Horsfall

James Horsfall

Scott & Vickie Horsfall

Tim Hughes

Glen Iwasaki

Sunil Jain

Frank Jennings

Joke and Biagio Productions

Eric Koester

Warren Laine-Naida

John Lund

Marta Maraboli

Teddy Matayoshi

Megan McDonald &
Kevin O'Keefe

Lori McNee

Marty & Misty McPadden

Fiorenza Mella

Mitch Mitchell

Michael Mogelgaard

David & Carol Nakamura

Melissa Nakamura

Mike Nakamura

Leslie Newman

Kane Nickolichuk

PierLuigi Ogliaro

Mike Olver

Steven & Priscilla Otsuki

Wayne & Katrine Otsuki

Karen Padrick

Laura Perry

Michelle Peterson

Doug Plummer

Lynn Purdy

Bridget Raftery

Alessandro Rea

Mardie Rhodes

Mike Simon

Smemail2

Peggy Soong-Yaplee

Carol Stephen

Karl Stillman

Christer Swaretz

Kristi Tanodra

Barbara & Chet Thayer

Brenda Thayer

Colette Tracy

Kim Traverse

Monica Vila

Pat Weaver

Bill Whetstone

Bridget Willard

Midge Williams

David Wong

Paula Wong

Robert Yalung

Flora Yang

My small army of beta readers gave me essential feedback to make my book better. I'm deeply indebted to David Horsfall, Carol Nakamura, Melissa Nakamura, and Linda Smith.

To my subject-matter experts and other early readers, including Kyle Barber, Nancy Boysen, Deke Bridges, Matt Carracino, Ron Elgin, Tim Hughes, Ron Lichty, Lori McNee, Mike Simon, and Carol Stephen, I thank you to infinity and beyond.

My husband David and son Charley were more supportive and patient than I deserved, and I'm very grateful.

Thanks to my Instagram friends who contributed and participated. Your names appear throughout the pages of this book. Thanks also to Emily Birchfield, Robin Frederick, Jan Gordon, Chris Brogan, Louis Menand, B.J. Mendelson, and Neal Schaffer, who helped me during the early stages of writing.

There are tons of people with Creators Institute and New Degree Press who helped me get here. Special thanks to my editor, John Chancey, publisher Brian Bies, early editors Jordana Megonigal, Blake Hoena, and Allison Tovey and the copy editors, designers and production people who worked on my book. Props to Zoran Maksimović, who endeavored through a challenging layout and Novak Dimitrovski who did a great job with design. I've been there and appreciate your contributions.

Most importantly, sincere thanks to friends and followers in my Instagram community. It's because of your interactions and encouragement that I dared to pursue my dream. There are roughly 450 friends whose engagement kicked off the idea for writing *Blogging on Instagram*. To all of you who are reading this and recognize yourselves, (((HUGS))) and thank you.

Terri Nakamura
Seattle, Washington
28 June 2021
@terrinakamura on Instagram

RESOURCES

———

There are many more apps and options, but here are some that may be helpful to you. (Live links as of June 15, 2021.)

CONTENT CREATION APPS—MOBILE
BRAINY QUOTES
https://apps.apple.com/us/app/brainyquote-famous-quotes/id916307096

CANVA
iOS
https://apps.apple.com/us/app/canva-graphic-design-video/id897446215

Android
https://play.google.com/store/apps/details?id=com.canva.editor&hl=en_US&gl=US

CRELLO
https://crello.com/about-crello/
(links to iOS and Android apps on the website)

LIGHTROOM

iOS

https://apps.apple.com/us/app/
adobe-lightroom-photo-editor/id878783582

Android

https://play.google.com/store/apps/details?id=com.adobe.lrmobile

PICQUOTES

Android

https://play.google.com/store/apps/details?id=com.
km.picturequotes

Pixlr on iOS, Android and web

iOS

https://apps.apple.com/us/app/pixlr-photo-collages-effect/
id526783584

Android

https://play.google.com/store/apps/details?id=com.pixlr.
express

PHONTO

https://apps.apple.com/ae/app/phonto-text-on-photos/
id438429273

PHOTO EDITOR ON IOS

PRISMA

iOS

https://apps.apple.com/us/app/prisma-photo-editor/
id1122649984

Android
https://play.google.com/store/apps/details?id=com.
neuralprisma

QUOTES CREATOR
iOS
https://apps.apple.com/bj/app/quotes-creator-quote-maker/
id895331100

Android
https://play.google.com/store/apps/details?id=com.ist.
quotescreator&hl=en_US

SNAPSEED
iOS
https://apps.apple.com/us/app/snapseed/id439438619

Android
https://play.google.com/store/apps/details?id=com.niksoft-
ware.snapseed

TEXT 2 PIC - $4.99
iOS
https://apps.apple.com/us/app/text2pic-add-
text-to-photos-poster-maker-logo-creator/
id536817268

Android
https://baixarapk.gratis/en/app/536817268/
text2pic-text-on-photos

VSCO
iOS
https://apps.apple.com/us/app/vsco-photo-video-editor/
id588013838

Android
https://play.google.com/store/apps/details?id=com.vsco.cam

WERBLE
iOS
https://apps.apple.com/us/app/
werble-photo-video-animator/id966009633

WORD SWAG
iOS
https://apps.apple.com/us/app/word-swag-cool-fonts/
id645746786
(available on Android but the reviews are not great!)

CONTENT CREATION WEB-BASED RESOURCES
Some are available on mobile.

ADOBE SPARK
https://spark.adobe.com/

BEFUNKY
https://www.befunky.com/features/graphic-designer/

BRAINY QUOTES
https://www.brainyquote.com/topics/image-quotes

CANVA

https://www.canva.com/

CRELLO

https://crello.com/about-crello/

DESIGN WIZARD

https://www.designwizard.com/

FOTOR

https://www.fotor.com/

GOODREADS:

https://www.goodreads.com/quotes/tag/inspirational

PABLO BY BUFFER

https://pablo.buffer.com/

PIXLR

https://pixlr.com/desktop/

QUOTESCOVER IMAGE MAKER

https://quotescover.com/

QUOTESGRAM

https://quotesgram.com/
copyright-free-inspirational-quotes/

QUOZIO

http://quozio.com/

RIPL

https://www.ripl.com/

SNAPPA

https://snappa.com/

STENCIL

https://getstencil.com/

TYLE.IO

https://tyle.io/

STOCK PHOTOGRAPHY AND MORE (LOW COST)
Please check fees, licensing, and usage.

123RF

https://www.123rf.com/

ADOBE STOCK

https://stock.adobe.com/

BIGSTOCK PHOTOS

https://www.bigstockphoto.com/

CANVA

https://www.canva.com/

DEATH TO STOCK

https://deathtothestockphoto.com/

DEPOSIT PHOTOS

https://depositphotos.com/

DREAMSTIME

https://www.dreamstime.com/

ISTOCKPHOTO

https://www.istockphoto.com/

SHUTTERSTOCK

https://www.shutterstock.com/

STOCK PHOTOGRAPHY RESOURCES (FREE OR CC0)

CC0 indicates a Creative Commons License. Other licensing is noted.

FOCA (SEARCHABLE, CC0)

https://focastock.com/

FOODIES FEED (SEARCHABLE, CC0)

https://www.foodiesfeed.com/

FREESTOCKS – (SEARCHABLE, CC0)

https://freestocks.org/

FREE RANGE STOCK (SEARCHABLE; LICENSING VIA EQUALICENSE -

https://freerangestock.com/

(License info: https://www.equalicense.com/)

GRATISOGRAPHY (SEARCHABLE; FREE VIA
GRATISPHOTOGRAPHY LICENSE)
https://gratisography.com/

ISOREPUBLIC (SEARCHABLE, CC0)
https://isorepublic.com/

KABOOMPICS (SEARCHABLE; FREE; CHECK FAQS
https://kaboompics.com/
(License info: https://kaboompics.com/page/license-and-faq)

LIFEOFPIX (SEARCHABLE; FREE TO USE)
https://www.lifeofpix.com/

LITTLEVISUALS (NOT SEARCHABLE; INTERESTING STORY; FREE TO USE)
https://littlevisuals.co/

JAY MANTRI (NOT SEARCHABLE; CC0)
https://jaymantri.com/

MORGUEFILE (SEARCHABLE; FREE TO USE)
https://morguefile.com/

NEGATIVESPACE (SEARCHABLE, CC0)
https://negativespace.co/

PEXELS (SEARCHABLE; CC0)
https://www.pexels.com/

PICJUMBO (SEARCHABLE; FREE TO USE, BUT CHECK
https://picjumbo.com/
(License info: https://picjumbo.com/faq-and-terms/)

PICOGRAPHY (SEARCHABLE, CC0)
https://picography.co/

PICSPREE (SEARCHABLE, TERMS)
https://picspree.com/en
(License info: https://picspree.com/en/pages/terms)

PIXABAY (SEARCHABLE, CC0)
https://pixabay.com/

RESHOT (SEARCHABLE, FREE VIA RESHOT LICENSE)
https://www.reshot.com/

SKITTERPHOTO (SEARCHABLE, CC0)
https://skitterphoto.com/

STOCKSNAP (SEARCHABLE – CC0)
https://stocksnap.io/

UNSPLASH (SEARCHABLE; UNSPLASH LICENSE)
https://unsplash.com/

WATERMARK APPS
A+ SIGNATURE
iOS
https://apps.apple.com/us/app/a-signature/id409956176

ADD WATERMARK ON PHOTOS
Android
https://play.google.com/store/apps/details?id=com.Simply-Entertaining.addwatermark&hl=en

EZY WATERMARK LITE

iOS

https://apps.apple.com/us/app/ezy-watermark-photos-lite/
id494473910

Android

https://play.google.com/store/apps/details?id=com.whiz-pool.ezywatermarklite&hl=en

IWATERMARK

iOS

https://apps.apple.com/us/app/
iwatermark-watermark-photos/id357577420

Android

https://play.google.com/store/apps/details?id=com.plumamazingfree.iwatermark

MARKSTA

iOS

https://apps.apple.com/us/app/marksta/id589118011

WATERMARK X

iOS

https://apps.apple.com/us/app/
watermark-x-copyright-photo-s/id1100583565

Android

http://androidapk-s.com/app/1100583565/
watermark-x-copyright-photo-s

UMARK PHOTO WATERMARKER

Mac
https://www.uconomix.com/Downloads.aspx

Windows
https://www.uconomix.com/Downloads.aspx

iOS
https://www.uconomix.com/Downloads.aspx

Android
https://www.uconomix.com/Downloads.aspx

GLOSSARY

———

This is a list of some of the words and terms I've mentioned in the preceding pages. I've defined them to reflect my use in this book. More comprehensive definitions can be found by searching the web.

Affiliate Marketing
Promotion of a product or service through a specific link where a commission is paid to the posting entity (e.g., blogger or website) following a sale.

Affiliate links
A specific link that drives and records traffic to an advertiser's website.

Algorithm
A set of calculations that solves a problem. Currently Instagram's algorithm determines which content is made the most visible, and the order in which posts are shown to users.

Avatar or Profile Picture
A photo or visual representation of you and your account.

Backlinks
Links that connect one domain to another, reinforcing the authority of a site. Assists with SEO.

Bio or Biography
A short summary that includes your username and handle or moniker (@name) contact information, hashtags, and usually a link.

Blog
A web page or website containing articles or personal commentary that is regularly updated.

Blog post
Writing or other content published on a blog.

Blogger
A person who writes or produces content shared to a blog.

Boomerang
A burst of photos stitched together to create a short, looping video, using the Boomerang app.

Bots
A software program that automates repetitive tasks.

Brand
A person, company or product, and the perceptions formed based on their content and profile.

Captions
A written description or story that accompanies your photos and other visual content.

Carousel
A type of post that shares up to ten photos or videos at once.

Click farm
A location that generates traffic in bulk, performing clicks, likes and other functions.

Close Friends
A subset of your Instagram followers list who can view your private Instagram Stories.

Comments
Words, emojis, or other responses to your post.

Contacts
People who are in the contact list on your device.

Content Creation
The creation of content that is shared primarily online, including writing, photography, videography, constructing, or preparing posts that align with the goals of a user or brand.

Content Marketing
A strategic approach to create and distribute relevant content that informs, engages, entertains, and creates goodwill with the target audience.

Conversion
The result of getting readers to take the desired action, such as requesting a download, signing up for a newsletter, asking for more information, or making a purchase.

Creative Commons
A nonprofit organization that helps enable the sharing of creative properties for public use.

Cross-Posting
The sharing of a piece of content to more than one online destination.

CTA or Call to Action
The catalyst in your post that gets readers to take an action.

Dashboards
Management tools that integrate a variety of functions through a single interface.

Disruption
A radical change due to existing goods and services that come about through innovation.

DM or Direct Message
A private message sent directly to a person or group that is not openly visible.

E-commerce
The online buying and selling of goods and services.

Emojis
Pictograms used in electronic messages and web pages.

Engagement
Two-way interaction between users that leads to building connections.

Engagement writing
Writing to intentionally draw interaction with your audience.

Explore page
Curated content specific to each user, shown based on user preferences and interactions.

Fakes
Fictitious social media accounts available for purchase, created to inflate a user's following.

Feed
The content you see when you log in to Instagram. The content you post may appear on the feeds of your followers.

Followers
The list of users who follow you on Instagram.

FTC requirements
Federal Trade Commission expectations of disclosure to show when a user shares a post that is in exchange for goods, services, or payment.

Geotag or location tag
An electronic tag that identifies the place where a photo has been taken.

Grid
The visual layout of posts on your Instagram profile page, based on rows of three images usually separated by white gutters or spaces between each photo.

Hashtags
A word or phrase preceded by the hash (#) symbol that signals the contents of your post.

Image types
Photos, videos, animations, nonpictorial content, quotes, text-as-art, and any content shared in the image space of a post.

Impressions
The number of times your content has been seen.

Influencer
A user with the ability to persuade others through their authenticity and reach. Levels: Nano (1,000-10K followers); Micro (10K-100K followers); Macro (100K-1M followers); Mega (1M+ followers).

Insights
An overview of your account's reach, interactions, follower breakdown, top locations of your followers, age range, genders, and their most active times.

Insights on a post
The number of likes, comments, shares, saves, impressions, reach, and follows on an individual post.

Instagram Live
Instagram's "live streaming" video content option.

Instagram Reels
Short video clips that can incorporate added effects and be set to music. (Instagram's version of TikTok.)

Instagram Stories
Ephemeral 24-hour-lifespan content made up of videos, photos, text, music, and other interactive elements. (Instagram's version of Snapchat.)

Instagram TV or IGTV
Videos from one to fifteen minutes in length with automatic closed captions. (Instagram's version of YouTube.)

Likes
Approval of content shown by tapping a "heart" icon.

Links or hyperlinks
Allows navigation between websites and pages, and points to other pages, websites, and email addresses.

Mention
A method to get attention by including a username (@name) in your caption or post. Those mentioned are notified.

Metadata
Invisible data embedded in photos that can include the author, when the image was created or modified, the file size, and the type of device used to take a photo.

Microblogging platforms
Twitter, Instagram, Facebook, Tumblr, and other sites where users post short, frequent updates.

Niche
The category or the visual classification of your content, e.g., gardening, animals, landscapes, etc.

Owned media or owned space
Online properties such as a blog, website, or podcast that are owned and controlled by a user, brand, or company.

Profile
A short description of up to 150 characters in length that says who you are, what you do, where you're located, and how you can be contacted.

Profile picture or Avatar
An image that represents your account that becomes recognizable to users. Individuals often use photos of themselves. Brands use their logos as their profile pictures.

Reach
The number of users that viewed your post or story on a given day.

Rented media or rented space
Channels such as YouTube, Instagram, or Tumblr where users post content, but don't own the media and can't control what happens.

Rights Manager
The Facebook Rights Manager helps users manage images and identifies if a photo used as content violates copyright.

Save
The ability to add content to your collection by tapping the "ribbon" icon on the right below the post. You can view an archive of what you've saved.

Search engines
A program such as Firefox, Google, and Safari that searches databases for corresponding keywords throughout the Internet.

SEO
Search engine optimization is used on blogs and websites to increase the chances of a post turning up in search.

Shadowban
Blocking a user on a social media site without their knowledge, rendering their posts and content invisible to others.

Share
Amplification of another user's content by sharing to your Instagram Stories or reposting another user's content onto your feed. (Also see "cross-posting.")

Sponsored posts
A type of native ad published by an influencer who receives goods, services, or payment in exchange for their post. Also known as a promoted post.

Stock photography
Photographs that are available to use through a license.

Subscription
A method of building traffic to a blog.

Tagging
A method to identify people in a photo or post where their name is mentioned, and they are notified.

Teaser
The introduction to the post.

Theme
The category or visual niche of your content, e.g., gardening, animals, landscapes, etc.

Timeline
The order of the posts shown to you in your feed. In 2016, the timeline showed posts in chronological order from most recent to oldest. It's now dictated by the algorithm.

TLD or top-level domain
Domains at the highest level of the Internet naming system, e.g., dot.com, dot.net, dot.org.

Transparency
Showing authenticity and honesty about who you are.

UGC or user-generated content
Unpaid advertising through content posted by users. It reinforces brands and products through sharing content and tagging the brand or brand hashtags.

URL
Uniform resource locator, also known as a web address.

Views
A metric that reflects how well a video performs.

Watermark
Adding a name or © to images as a measure asserting ownership and rights.

APPENDIX

——

INTRODUCTION

Canning, Nikki. "The State of Instagram Influencer Marketing (+ Free Report)." *Later Blog,* December 9, 2019. https://later.com/blog/instagram-influencer-marketing-report/

CHAPTER 1
THE PATH TO BLOGGING

Albee, Ardath. In *Digital Relevance: Developing Marketing Content and Strategies That Drive Results.*New York: Palgrave Macmillan, 2015.

Bedingfield, Will. "The Rise and Fall of Flash, the Annoying Plugin That Shaped the Modern Web." *Wired UK,* September 18 2019. https://www.wired.co.uk/article/history-of-macromedia-flash.

Bizzul, Kali. "How Internal & External Linking Best Practices Build Your Blog." Verblio Blog, April 9, 2020. https://www.verblio.com/blog/internal-external-linking-best-practices-blog.

Kemp, Simon. "Digital 2021: Global Overview Report - DataReportal – Global Digital Insights." *DataReportal,* January 27, 2021. https://datareportal.com/reports/digital-2021-global-overview-report.

Kim, Larry. "What's a Good Conversion Rate? (It's Higher Than You Think)." *WordStream* (blog). Last updated, August 5, 2020. https://www.wordstream.com/blog/ws/2014/03/17/what-is-a-good-conversion-rate.

Pulizzi, Joe. "Seth Godin: 'Content Marketing Is the Only Marketing Left' and 10 New Marketing Lessons." *Content Marketing Institute,* January 14, 2008. https://contentmarketinginstitute.com/2008/01/seth-godin-cont/.

Schneider, Dave. "5 Smart Blogging Goals To Set Today." *Neal Schaffer* (blog). Last updated April 30, 2021. https://nealschaffer.com/5-smart-blogging-goals-set-2016/.

Tankovska, H. "Tumblr: Total Number of Blogs 2020." *Statista.* January 27, 2021. https://www.statista.com/statistics/256235/total-cumulative-number-of-tumblr-blogs/.

CHAPTER 2
ARE BLOGS STILL RELEVANT?

Brownstein Hyatt Farber Schreck. "FTC Issues New Guidelines for Social Media Influencers, Brands." *JD Supra,* January 28, 2020. https://www.jdsupra.com/legalnews/ftc-issues-new-guidelines-for-social-40544/.

Campbell, W. Joseph. "The 15 'Most Influential' Web Sites? A Third of Them Date to 1995." *The 1995 Blog.* October 4, 2017. https://1995blog.com/2017/10/24/the-15-most-influential-web-sites-a-third-of-them-date-to-1995/.

Facebook. "Will my Instagram profile be indexed on the web?" Instagram help. Last modified May, 2021. https://www.facebook.com/help/instagram/587098141302117 .

Hughes, Tim, and Matt Reynolds. "Five Steps to Getting You Started." In *Social Selling: Techniques to Influence Buyers and Changemakers,* 89. London: Kogan Page, 2016.

Mohsin, Maryam. "10 YouTube Stats Every Marketer Should Know in 2021 [Infographic]." *Oberlo* (blog). Oberlo. January 25, 2021. https://www.oberlo.com/blog/youtube-statistics.

Pulizzi, Joe. "Seth Godin: 'Content Marketing Is the Only Marketing Left' and 10 New Marketing Lessons." *Content Marketing Institute,* January 14, 2008. https://contentmarketinginstitute.com/2008/01/seth-godin-cont/.

Rainie, Lee. "The State of Blogging." Pew Research Center. May 30, 2005. https://www.pewresearch.org/internet/2005/01/02/the-state-of-blogging/.

Rastas, Johannes. "Affiliate Marketing Trends in 2021." Supermetrics, January 26, 2021. https://supermetrics.com/blog/affiliate-marketing-trends-2021.

Sanders, Konrad. "Is Blogging Finally Dead?" *Blog Tyrant*. Last updated August 6, 2020. https://www.blogtyrant.com/is-blogging-finally-dead/.

Sifry, David. "State of the Blogosphere, August 2006." *David Sifry* (blog). August 7, 2006. http://david-sifry-wrgy.squarespace.com/alerts/2006/08/state-of-the-blogosphere-august-2006

Spamhaus. "The 10 Most Abused Top Level Domains." Accessed June 18, 2021. https://www.spamhaus.org/statistics/tlds/.

Chapman, Cameron "A Brief History of Blogging." Webdesigner Depot. March 14, 2011. https://www.webdesignerdepot.com/2011/03/a-brief-history-of-blogging/.

CHAPTER 3
WHAT IS ENGAGEMENT WRITING?

Ayres, Scott. "Shocking New Data about the Lifespan of Your Facebook Posts." *Post Planner* (blog), December 2, 2016. https://www.postplanner.com/lifespan-of-facebook-posts/.

Bernazzani, Sophia. "13 Clever Ways to Get More Comments on Instagram This Month." *HubSpot* (blog), updated November 17, 2020. https://blog.hubspot.com/marketing/comments-on-instagram.

Epipheo. "What Is The Lifespan Of Social Media Posts?" Epipheo. Accessed May 26, 2021. https://epipheo.com/learn/what-is-the-lifespan-of-social-media-posts/.

InstaPro. "Why Your Like to Follower Ratio Matters on Instagram." *Edsocialmedia* (blog), April 25, 2019. https://edsocialmedia.org/why-your-like-to-follower-ratio-matters-on-instagram/.

Lorenz, Taylor. "How Comments Became the Best Part of Instagram." *The Atlantic,* January 4, 2019. https://www.theatlantic.com/technology/archive/2019/01/how-comments-became-best-part-instagram/579415/.

West, Chloe. "How to Get Traffic from Twitter That Converts." *Sprout Blog. Sprout Social,* January 22, 2020 https://sproutsocial.com/insights/twitter-traffic/.

CHAPTER 4
REAL-LIFE ENGAGEMENT WRITING

Boston University. "Handwritten Letters as a Revolutionary Communication Tool." Boston University Center for Mobile Communication Studies, September 14, 2018. https://sites.bu.edu/cmcs/2018/09/14/handwritten-letters-as-a-revolutionary-communication-tool/.

Mental Floss. "15 Forgotten Niceties We Should Bring Back." Accessed June 13, 2021. https://www.mentalfloss.com/article/86043/15-forgotten-niceties-we-should-bring-back.

Methot, Jessica R., Allison S. Gabriel, Patrick Downes, and Emily Rosado-Solomon. "Remote Workers Need Small Talk, Too." *Harvard Business Review,* March 25, 2021. https://hbr.org/2021/03/remote-workers-need-small-talk-too.

Nakamura, Terri. "Racing Bigfoot in the Shadow of Mount St. Helens." *Stories, Social Media & Tech*(blog). September 29, 2015. https://terri-nakamura.com/2015/09/29/racing-bigfoot/.

Pausch, Randy, and Jeffrey Zaslow. *The Last Lecture.* New York, NY: Hachette Books, 2018.

CHAPTER 5
RULES OF ENGAGEMENT

Balkthi, Syed. "How to Dramatically Improve Your Email Marketing in 4 Steps." *Instapage* (blog), January 16, 2020. https://instapage.com/blog/how-to-improve-email-marketing.

Johnson, Holly. "The 8 Best Social Media Management Software of 2021." Investopedia, last updated May 25, 2021. https://www.investopedia.com/best-social-media-management-software-5087716.

Morrow, Jon. "14 Devious Tactics for Getting More Comments on Your Blog Posts." Smart Blogger, May 8, 2020. https://smartblogger.com/more-comments/.

Oli. "Click Farms: What Are They & What Are They For?" *ClickCease* (blog), March 25, 2021. https://www.clickcease.com/blog/click-farms-what-are-they-what-are-they-for/.

Sahni, Navdeep S., S. Christian Wheeler, and Pradeep K. Chintanguta. "Personalization in Email Marketing: The Role of Non-Informative Advertising Content." SGSB Working Paper 3409, Stanford Graduate School of Business, October 23, 2016. https://www.gsb.stanford.edu/faculty-research/working-papers/personalization-email-marketing-role-non-informative-advertising.

Sehl, Katie. "14 Tips for Building a Multilingual Social Media Presence." *HootSuite* (blog), January 22, 2019. https://blog.hootsuite.com/multilingual-social-media-presence/.

Smigiera, M. "Most Spoken Languages in the World." Statista, March 30, 2021. https://www.statista.com/statistics/266808/the-most-spoken-languages-worldwide/.

Warren, Jillian. "Instagram Tests New Feature for Users to Hide Likes." *Later* (blog), May 20, 2021. https://later.com/blog/hidden-likes-instagram/.

CHAPTER 6
INSTAGRAM AS A DIGITAL DIARY

Cassata, Cathy. "How to Stop Feeling Lonely." Psych Central, April 26, 2021. https://psychcentral.com/lib/stop-feeling-lonely#how-to-stop-feeling-lonely.

Hdez, Gabriela. "Interesting Facts about Leonardo Da Vinci's Journals." Owlcation, February 29, 2020. https://owlcation.com/humanities/Interesting-Facts-about-Leonardo-Da-Vincis-Journals.

University of Rochester Medical Center. "Journaling for Mental Health." Health Encyclopedia. Accessed May 31, 2021. https://www.urmc.rochester.edu/encyclopedia/content.aspx?ContentID=4552&ContentTypeID=1.

Menand, Louis. "Woke Up This Morning." *The New Yorker,* December 2, 2007. https://www.newyorker.com/magazine/2007/12/10/woke-up-this-morning.

Tartakovsky, Margarita. "30 Journaling Prompts for Self-Reflection and Self-Discovery." Psych Central, September 27, 2014. https://psychcentral.com/blog/30-journaling-prompts-for-self-reflection-and-self-discovery#1.

CHAPTER 7
WHY BLOG ON INSTAGRAM?

Ackerman, Courtney E. "Writing Therapy: Using A Pen and Paper to Enhance Personal Growth." PositivePsychology, last updated March 22, 2021. https://positivepsychology.com/writing-therapy/.

Baadsgaard, Jacob. "How to Improve Your Conversion Rate By 50% in One Day." *Neil Patel* (blog), accessed June 2, 2021. https://neilpatel.com/blog/improve-your-conversion-rate-50-percent/.

Byers, Kyle. "How Many Blogs Are There? (And 141 Other Blogging Stats)." GrowthBadger, last updated January 23, 2021. https://growthbadger.com/blog-stats/.

Chacon, Benjamin. "Instagram SEO: 6 Ways to Increase Your Discoverability." Later Blog. July 29, 2020. https://later.com/blog/instagram-seo/.

Canning, Nikki. "The State of Instagram Influencer Marketing (+ Free Report)." Later Blog, December 8, 2019. https://later.com/blog/instagram-influencer-marketing-report/.

Christensen, Clayton M., Michael E. McDonald, and Rory McDonald. "What Is Disruptive Innovation?" *Harvard Business Review*, December 2015. https://hbr.org/2015/12/what-is-disruptive-innovation.

Ion, Florence. "Instagram Is Testing Story Links for All." *Gizmodo*, June 29, 2021. https://gizmodo.com/instagram-is-testing-story-links-for-all-1847195903.

Perez, Sarah. "Facebook and Instagram Will Now Allow Users to Hide 'Like' Counts on Posts." TechCrunch, May 26, 2021. https://techcrunch.com/2021/05/26/facebook-and-instagram-will-now-allow-users-to-hide-like-counts-on-posts/.

Pope, Lauren. "8 Little-Known Instagram SEO Techniques for Increasing Reach." HubSpot Blog, last updated October 25, 2019. https://blog.hubspot.com/marketing/instagram-seo.

Smith, M. Cecil. "The Benefits of Writing." Center for the Interdisciplinary Study of Language and Literacy. Northern Illinois University, n.d.. https://www.niu.edu/language-literacy/_pdf/the-benefits-of-writing.pdf.

CHAPTER 8
CREATING YOUR PERSONAL BRAND

Bond, Conor. "The 34 Best Instagram Bios the Internet Has Ever Seen." WordStream. Last updated May 10, 2021. https://www.wordstream.com/blog/ws/2020/04/09/instagram-bios.

Hilder, Rosie. "5 Steps to an Irresistible Instagram Bio." Creative Bloq. October 25, 2019. https://www.creativebloq.com/features/instagram-bio.

Gravatar. "What is Gravatar?" Accessed May 29, 2021. https://en.gravatar.com/support/what-is-gravatar.

Olafson, Karin, and Tony Tran. "Social Media Image Sizes 2021: Cheat Sheet for Every Network." *Hootsuite* (blog). December 11, 2020. https://blog.hootsuite.com/social-media-image-sizes-guide/#Instagram_image_sizes.

Simpson, Matt. "How To: Get Instagram Traffic to Show Up in Google Analytics." Magnetic Creative. August 2, 2019. https://www.magneticcreative.com/journal/instagram-traffic-in-google-analytics/.

West, Chloe. "Why and How to Set up Your Instagram Business Profile." Sprout Social. August 6, 2020. https://sproutsocial.com/insights/instagram-business-profile/.

CHAPTER 9
IF YOU BUILD IT, THEY WILL COME

Barnhart, Brent. "The Most Important Instagram Statistics You Need to Know for 2021." Sprout Social, February 25, 2021. https://sproutsocial.com/insights/instagram-stats/.

Bates, Kelly. "13 Most Popular Types of Instagram Photos That Will Get You More Likes and Followers." Pixobo, accessed June 7, 2021. https://www.pixobo.com/popular-types-of-instagram-photos/.

Elsley, Sam. "3 Reasons You Should Respond to Instagram Comments ASAP." Mondovo Blog, accessed June 7, 2021. https://www.mondovo.com/blog/3-reasons-you-should-respond-to-instagram-comments-asap/.

Gotter, Ana. "The 29 Instagram Statistics You Need to Know in 2021."
AdEspresso Blog, April 21, 2021.
https://adespresso.com/blog/instagram-statistics/.

Heath, Chip. "Made to Stick Quotes by Chip Heath." Goodreads.
Accessed June 7, 2021.
https://www.goodreads.com/work/quotes/1472304.

Later and Fohr. "The State of Influencer Marketing in 2020." Accessed
May 31, 2021.
https://later-com.s3.amazonaws.com/ebooks/Later-Fohr-StateofInstag
ramInfluencerMarketing2020.pdf.

Lee, Andrew. "Instagram Shadowban (2021): What It Is And How To
Remove It." *Andrew Lee Ventures*(blog). March 1, 2021.
https://andrewlee.ventures/blog/instagram-shadowban-what-it-is-and-
how-to-remove-it.

Michalski, Justina. "Instagram Study 2019: What We Learned
Analyzing 5.4 Million Posts." Quintly Blog, September 9, 2019.
https://www.quintly.com/blog/instagram-study-2019.

Newberry, Christina. "The 2020 Instagram Hashtag Guide—How to
Use Them and Get Results." Hootsuite, June 23, 2020.
https://blog.hootsuite.com/instagram-hashtags/.

Newton, Casey. "What Instagram Really Learned from Hiding like
Counts." *The Verge*, May 27, 2021.
https://www.theverge.com/2021/5/27/22456206/instagram-hiding-likes-
experiment-results-platformer.

Warren, Jillian. "The Ultimate Guide to Writing Good Instagram
Captions." Later Blog, July 25, 2019.
https://later.com/blog/the-ultimate-guide-to-writing-good-
instagram-captions/.

CHAPTER 10
LIGHTS, CAMERA, ACTION!

Bernardini, Gabrielle. "Was the Carousel Feature Deleted on
Instagram? Fans Are Worried After the Icon Is Seemingly Missing."
Distractify. May 21, 2021.
https://www.distractify.com/p/how-to-post-multiple-photos-on-instagram.

Glover, George. "5 Reasons to Embrace and Invest in IGTV and How to
Do It Well." Quintly, August 26, 2020.
https://www.quintly.com/blog/5-reasons-to-embrace-and-invest-in-
igtv-and-how-to-do-it-well.

McLachlan, Stacey. "Instagram Story Hacks: 32 Tricks and Features You Should Know." Hootsuite Blog, June 1, 2021. https://blog.hootsuite.com/instagram-story-hacks/.

Pearce, Hayley. "Why Carousels Beat Videos in the Social Media Engagement Game." Productsup Blog, February 16, 2021. https://www.productsup.com/blog/why-carousels-beat-videos-social-media/.

Rev. "How to Add Captions & Subtitles to IGTV Videos." October 23, 2020. https://www.rev.com/blog/how-to-add-captions-subtitles-to-igtv-videos.

Schaffer, Neal. "The 27 Definitive Instagram Statistics for 2021 You Should Know - and Why." Neal Schaffer. Last updated, June 6, 2021. https://nealschaffer.com/instagram-statistics/.

Stanton, William. "How To Create a Boomerang for an Instagram Post or Story." *Alphr*, April 20, 2021. https://www.alphr.com/create-boomerang-instagram-post-story/.

Warren, Jillian. "The Ultimate Guide to IGTV." Later Blog, April 1, 2021. https://later.com/blog/igtv/.

West, Chloe. "Your Guide to Instagram Live for Business." Sprout Social, March 26, 2021. https://sproutsocial.com/insights/instagram-live/.

CHAPTER 11
FROM CAPTIONS TO CONTENT

Aslam, Salman. "Instagram by the Numbers: Stats, Demographics and Fun Facts." Omnicore Blog, last updated January 6, 2021. https://www.omnicoreagency.com/instagram-statistics/.

Canning, Nikki. "The State of Instagram Influencer Marketing (+ Free Report)." Later Blog, June 9, 2020. https://later.com/blog/instagram-influencer-marketing-report/.

Gotter, Ana. "The 29 Instagram Statistics You Need to Know in 2021." AdEspresso Blog, April 21, 2021. https://adespresso.com/blog/instagram-statistics/.

HubSpot. "Instagram Engagement Report." Accessed June 10, 2021. https://offers.hubspot.com/instagram-engagement-report-2021.

Jackson, Dominique. "Know Your Limit: The Ideal Length of Every Social Media Post." Sprout Social. December 15, 2020. https://sproutsocial.com/insights/social-media-character-counter/.

Later+Fohr. Rep. *The State of Influencer Marketing in 2020*. Later+Fohr. Accessed May 31, 2021. https://later-com.s3.amazonaws.com/ebooks/Later-Fohr-StateofInstag ramInfluencerMarketing2020.pdf.

Michalski, Justina. "Instagram Study 2019: What We Learned Analyzing 5.4 Million Posts." Quintly Blog, September 9, 2019. https://www.quintly.com/blog/instagram-study-2019.

Mohsin, Maryam. "10 Instagram Stats Every Marketer Should Know in 2021 [Infographic]." Oberlo Blog, February 16, 2021. https://www.oberlo.com/blog/instagram-stats-every-marketer-should-know.

Newberry, Christina. "25 YouTube Statistics That May Surprise You: 2021 Edition." Hootsuite Blog, February 2, 2021. https://blog.hootsuite.com/youtube-stats-marketers/.

Ross, Harling. "Investigating the Long Captions on Instagram Trend." Repeller, July 6, 2017. https://repeller.com/long-captions-on-instagram-trend/.

Sonnenberg, Anna. "The Lifespan of Social Media Content." Content Marketing Agency | Content Marketing Services by CopyPress, March 2, 2020. https://www.copypress.com/blog/lifespan-social-media-content/.

Vogue Magazine. "Photo of Raquel Willis." Instagram, June 30, 2020. Accessed June 20, 2021. https://www.instagram.com/p/CCEyurgFQtF/?utm_source=ig_ web_copy_link

CHAPTER 12
MAKE YOUR FEED AWESOME

Cho, Mikael. "Unsplash Is Being Acquired by Getty Images." Unsplash. March 30, 2021. https://unsplash.com/blog/unsplash-getty/.

Creative Commons. "CC0 1.0 Universal (CC0 1.0) Public Domain Dedication." Accessed June 7, 2021. https://creativecommons.org/publicdomain/zero/1.0/.

Del Gigante, Michael. "Facebook Adds Video to Instagram." MDG Advertising. June 20, 2013. https://www.mdgadvertising.com/marketing-insights/facebook-adds-video-to-instagram/.

Link. "Top 9 (Free and Paid) Watermark Apps for Android & iPhone."
Link Blog, September 11, 2020.
https://blog.elink.io/free-and-paid-watermark-apps/.

Morey, Raelene. "How to Use Instagram Quote Maker Apps to Fill Your
Feed With Inspirational Quotes." Revive Social Blog, May 20, 2021.
https://revive.social/instagram-quote-maker/.

Sharma, Lucky. "Best Watermark Apps For Android Devices 2021."
The Android Portal, April 4, 2020.
https://www.theandroidportal.com/best-watermark-apps-for-android/.

CHAPTER 13
ARE YOU FEELING LUCKY?

Sachar, Louis, and Joel Schick. *Wayside School. Wayside School Is
Falling Down.* Boston: Lothrop, Lee and Shepard Books, 1989.

CHAPTER 14
TIPS FOR BUILDING COMMUNITY

AIGrow. "The Right Way to Use Follow Unfollow on Instagram." Accessed
June 14, 2021.
https://aigrow.me/follow-unfollow-instagram/.

Canning, Nikki. "11 Ways to Increase Instagram Engagement in 2021."
Later Blog, February 14, 2021.
https://later.com/blog/how-to-increase-instagram-engagement/.

Cooper, Paige. "I Tried Instagram Automation (So You Don't Have To):
An Experiment." Hootsuite Blog, May 4, 2020.
https://blog.hootsuite.com/i-tried-instagram-automation-so-you-dont-
have-to/.

HubSpot, and Mention. "Instagram Engagement Report." HubSpot.
Accessed June 10, 2021.
https://offers.hubspot.com/instagram-engagement-report-2021.

Juhola, Sebastian. "How I Grew an Instagram Account from 4000
Followers to 190k in a Year." Reddit, October 27, 2020.
https://www.reddit.com/r/Entrepreneur/comments/jj7vdr/how_i_
grew_an_instagram_account_from_4000/.

MacDonald, Mark. "How to Get More Followers on Instagram: 15 Reliable Ways to Grow Your Audience." Shopify Blog, August 3, 2020. https://www.shopify.com/blog/14288561-how-to-build-a-massive-following-on-instagram.

Roach, Andrew. "Instagram Engagement: What It Is and How to Improve It in 2021." Oberlo Blog, October 7, 2020. https://www.oberlo.com/blog/instagram-engagement-improve.

Social Pros. "Know and Beat Instagram's Daily Limits: 2021 Update." April 20, 2021. https://socialpros.co/instagram-daily-limits.

Emelina Spinelli. "Instagram Growth Hacks for Small Accounts | Organic Instagram Growth Hacks." January 21, 2020. Video, 5:18. https://www.youtube.com/watch?v=8Xe4iQw4N7Y.